CORE COMMUNICATION
Skills and Processes

Sherod Miller, Ph.D.
Phyllis A. Miller, Ph.D.

Cover design:
Barrie Maguire

Design Assistance:
Robert Bolenbaucher
Robert Friederichsen

Editorial Assistance:
Levi Miller

**INTERPERSONAL
COMMUNICATION
PROGRAMS, INC.**

**Suite 200
30772 Southview Drive
Evergreen, Colo. 80439
Phone: 1-800-328-5099
www.comskills.com**

PURPOSE

The purpose of *Core Communication* is to enhance your intrapersonal and interpersonal competence — your ability to:

■ Communicate (talk and listen) more effectively

■ Resolve issues/conflicts — inside yourself and with others — better

■ Facilitate issue/conflict resolution within another person or between people

As you achieve the purpose, you will be able to:

■ Expand your options for meeting and handling personal challenges

■ Create more satisfying relationships

■ Increase productivity when a task is involved

■ Build self-esteem and other-esteem

PRACTICAL APPLICATIONS

Core Communication applies directly to:

■ Solving problems

■ Making decisions

■ Resolving conflicts

■ Facilitating

■ Counseling

■ Managing

■ Coaching

■ Negotiating

■ Mediating

■ Influencing

OBJECTIVES

The specific objectives of *Core Communication* are for you to:

- Distinguish four styles of communication and recognize the impact of each style on the quality of information exchanged and the effect on relationships.
- Identify five parts of your awareness and recognize how those parts influence your interactions.
- Use six talking skills for sending clear, effective messages.
- Use five listening skills for understanding others and building relationships.
- Apply your awareness and the skills in processes for resolving issues and conflicts personally and interpersonally.
- Apply practical interactive principles and guides to create effective exchanges.
- Apply tools and coaching to improve your use of the skills and processes.

MATERIALS

Each participant uses his or her own Core Pac, which includes:

- This workbook — *Core Communication: Skills and Processes*
- One Awareness Wheel floor skills mat
- One Listening Cycle floor skills mat
- A set of pocket cards
- An Awareness Wheel pad

These materials aid learning during and between class sessions and guide continued application afterwards.

GROUND RULES

As you learn the skills and processes of this program, keep the following ground rules in mind.

■ Participate voluntarily in any activity (exercise) or discussion. If for any reason you do not choose to participate, say so. You can pass.

■ Respect boundaries. Every individual has his or her own informational boundaries. Take your own and others' into account. To do this:

　　1. Identify or choose issues you think are appropriate to talk about in this setting.

　　2. Do not pressure anyone else to disclose anything he or she does not wish to disclose.

■ Choose real issues, when possible, as you focus on skill practice. You may want to use small issues instead of major ones as you learn the skills and processes.

■ Assume you will be coached by the instructor and others in the class. Coaching and receiving feedback are essential for learning.

ACKNOWLEDGEMENTS

The authors wish to thank Daniel B. Wackman, Ph.D. and Elam W. Nunnally, Ph.D. for their contributions to the development and research of the ideas foundational to this workbook.

Other people who have influenced this work over the years include: Reuben Hill, Ph.D., Virginia Satir, Ph.D., William Fawcett Hill, Ph.D., Sidney Jourard, Ph.D., Gerhard Neubeck, Ed.D., and Richard Hey, Ph.D.

A special thanks to the ICP Instructors who have given encouragement, feedback, and suggestions valuable in the writing of this workbook.

CONTENTS

GAUGE YOUR PROGRESS

Date _____

Instructions: To allow you to gauge your progress, take this Pre-Questionnaire to assesses your current skill level. The questions relate to the skills and processes taught in *Core Communication*. Please follow the four steps below. Then set your learning goals on page xi.

> **Step 1.** Mark each item twice: first with an "X" to represent your typical behavior and again with an "O" to represent your more-so- or less-so desired behavior. If your typical and desired behaviors are the same, the "X" and "O" marks will be on the same number. If they are not the same, the marks will fall on different numbers.

In general, when you are discussing an issue with someone, how often do you:

	Seldom Often	Difference
1. Direct or instruct the other in what to do about it?	1 2 3 4 5 6	____
2. Blame or attack the other directly?	1 2 3 4 5 6	____
3. Send clear, complete, and straightforward messages?	1 2 3 4 5 6	____
4. Make spiteful, undercutting remarks indirectly?	1 2 3 4 5 6	____
5. Explore possible causes of the issue?	1 2 3 4 5 6	____
6. Speak for other — put words into the other's mouth?	1 2 3 4 5 6	____
7. Use your full awareness to reflect on the issue?	1 2 3 4 5 6	____
8. Share your feelings?	1 2 3 4 5 6	____
9. Disclose your wants and desires?	1 2 3 4 5 6	____
10. Calm yourself consciously when you feel tense or encounter tension in the other	1 2 3 4 5 6	____
11. Establish and maintain rapport?	1 2 3 4 5 6	____
12. Listen briefly, then begin talking?	1 2 3 4 5 6	____
13. Attend to the other's nonverbal responses?	1 2 3 4 5 6	____
14. Acknowledge the other's feelings?	1 2 3 4 5 6	____
15. Acknowledge the wants and desires of the other?	1 2 3 4 5 6	____
16. Invite/encourage the other to expand on a point of view?	1 2 3 4 5 6	____
17. Ask what the other is thinking, feeling, and wanting?	1 2 3 4 5 6	____

	Seldom	Often	Difference
18. Summarize messages of the other to ensure accuracy?	1 2 3 4 5 6		___
19. Avoid the issue by joking or changing the subject?	1 2 3 4 5 6		___
20. Force decisions on the other?	1 2 3 4 5 6		___
21. Give in to the other's decision?	1 2 3 4 5 6		___
22. Talk about the issue but leave it unresolved?	1 2 3 4 5 6		___
23. Settle the issue by compromising — trading for something?	1 2 3 4 5 6		___
24. Resolve the issue by building agreements collaboratively?	1 2 3 4 5 6		___
25. Identify clearly what the issue is before discussing it?	1 2 3 4 5 6		___
26. Begin a discussion without considering the other's readiness?	1 2 3 4 5 6		___
27. Propose a good time and place to discuss the issue?	1 2 3 4 5 6		___
28. Decide upon a solution before fully hearing the concern?	1 2 3 4 5 6		___
29. Brainstorm solutions to the issue?	1 2 3 4 5 6		___
30. Make sure a solution to the issue fits well for everyone involved?	1 2 3 4 5 6		___

Total Difference Score ___

Step 2. When you have completed marking all the items, calculate the numerical difference between typical and desired scores for each item and record the results in the "difference" column. If the "X" and "O" are on the same number, the difference = 0. If the "X" is on 5 and the "O" is on 2, the difference = 3. Note the the "O" can be located on a higher or lower number than the "X." Do not be concerned about the higher or lower direction of the scores, just calculate the numerical difference between the marks.

Step 3. Sum the difference scores (for Post-Questionnaire comparison).

Step 4. Look over the Questionnaire above and put a check mark next to each item number (to the left of a question) with a difference score of "2" or more. These relate to skills and processes most beneficial for you to develop or change. (See next page to set your learning goals.)

SET YOUR LEARNING GOALS

Instructions: From the items you checked on the pre-questionnaire (see Step 4 above), write five behaviors you want to increase or decrease. Consider these as your major learning goals.

Goals: **Brief description of behavior to increase or decrease:**

1. Item # ____   _____

2. Item # ____   _____

3. Item # ____   _____

4. Item # ____   _____

5. Item # ____   _____

After the course, take the post-questionnaire on page 155, to compare your change in awareness and skill.

WORKSHEET: SOMEONE YOU WANT TO INFLUENCE

Instructions: Think of a person you want to influence about something of importance to you. Time yourself; take four minutes, and in the space below, organize what you want to say to this person.

Person's name:_____

Later you will return to this page.

INTRODUCTION

The Third Force
The 80/20 Rule
It Takes One Person

THE THIRD FORCE

All of us face issues as we go about our daily living. An issue is anything (situation, event, experience, awareness, opportunity) that concerns us. It usually involves making a decision and often means resolving a conflict. Issues can be:

- Our own personal issues
- Conflicts with others
- Disputes that we try to settle between other people

The First Force — Content

When you find yourself in a situation that involves an issue, generally you immediately orient yourself to the *content* — what it concerns.

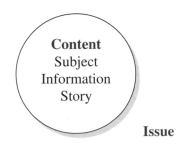

Issue

You wonder quickly: "What does this have to do with me?" "Is this of interest to me?" "How important is this?" "Do I have any experience in this area?" "Do I have time to participate?" "Do I have something to contribute?"

Content is a strong force. It can pull you into the situation, or it can cause you to try to move away. The more connected you are to the subject, the easier it is to lock on to content. You can be aware or unaware of important pieces of content regarding yourself or another person when an issue is involved.

The Second Force — Outcome

You deal with an issue to find a solution or to resolve a conflict — develop a satisfactory, workable *outcome*. And in the fast-paced world of today, a premium often exists on arriving at an outcome quickly.

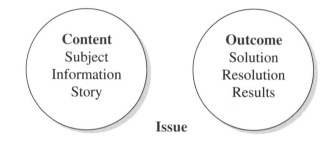

You respond: "Here's what to do." "This is the answer." "Try this." "Take this course of action." "Decide later."

Outcome is a powerful force, too. You attempt to determine (or sidestep) a resolution. This happens whether the issue is yours alone, yours with someone else, or someone's that you are trying to mediate. Sometimes the outcomes fit; many times they do not, and satisfaction drops.

With an issue at hand, our exchanges with others usually focus on content or end results — two forces. Gaining agreement about the significant content and the outcome needed takes on greatest importance, even if it must be forced. In these situations, if agreement

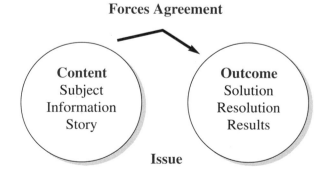

is not reached, resistance, pressure, and stress grow for everyone. Sometimes people get stuck, and their relationships are damaged.

The Third Force — Process

Process is the way you deal with content and develop an outcome regarding an issue. In all your exchanges with someone else (and even when you make decisions on your own), a process interplay goes on, whether or not you are aware of it.

Process is a third force that either supports or inhibits productive communication and satisfying issue resolution. A skilled, effective process facilitates quality content and workable outcomes that fit the situation. It pursues understanding as it works collaboratively to build agreements and consensus.

When you attend well to process — recognize its impact and put it to work for everyone involved — you can deal more effectively with complicated and difficult issues.

Core Communication aims to increase your awareness of process and to equip you with practical skills so you can better work out the issues you encounter throughout life. The book also provides interactive principles and guides to help you connect with others in more satisfying ways.

Forces Agreement

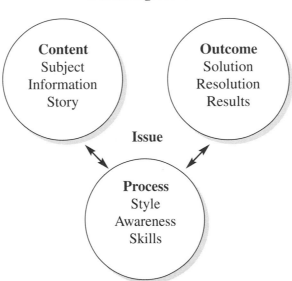

Pursues Understanding/Builds Agreement

ASSUMPTIONS

The concepts and skills presented in *Core Communication* are based on two assumptions:

AN 80/20 RULE: LOOK INSIDE FIRST

> *About 80 percent of the time, the important content for creating satisfying outcomes to the challenging issues you face resides inside yourself and the others involved.*

This rule of thumb applies to resolving:

- Your own personal issues
- Conflicts with others
- Disputes between other people, when you help facilitate a resolution

The 80/20 rule supports self-other awareness — the basis for *intra*personal and *inter*personal competence.

Many people operate in the reverse — from a 20/80 perspective. They look largely to information outside of themselves and the others involved as they deal with issues and resolve their conflicts.

The concepts and skills presented in *Core Communication* will help you improve how you connect with critical information inside yourself and others, as you negotiate differences and build satisfying, workable agreements.

IT TAKES ONE PERSON

> *It only takes one person to change an interaction.*

Many people wait for and expect someone else to change, in order to improve their communication. This often equals no change.

The assumption in this workbook is that you, on your own, can effectively apply skills and processes to influence your interactions positively, even if others do not know the skills.

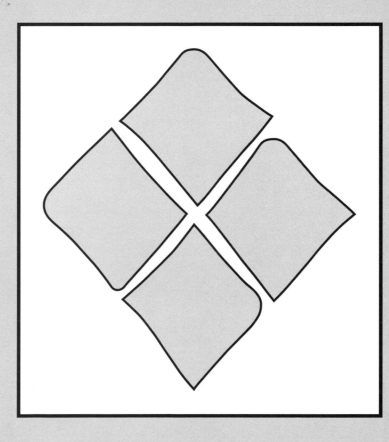

1

COMMUNICATION STYLES MAP

How You Talk and Listen

TALKING

Each time you say something, your message contains two parts:

- *What* you say — the content
- *How* you say it — the style

What you talk about makes a difference, yet your style — *how* you talk about something — has the greatest impact on your communication. Your verbal and nonverbal style is a command or relational message. It tells others the way to take your message about the content — to recognize that you are joking, angry, tentative, or serious.

LISTENING

Your style of listening influences an interaction, too. *How* you listen has a measurable effect on the quality of information the other person expresses.

Since people respond to *how* as much as they do to *what,* the outcome of a conversation varies significantly depending on the talking and listening styles you use in the exchange. The way you talk and listen either helps or interferes with your ability to connect with the other person. Many failures to communicate stem from the use of styles of communication inappropriate for the situation.

COMMUNICATION STYLES

How you talk and listen to someone falls into one of four major communication styles.

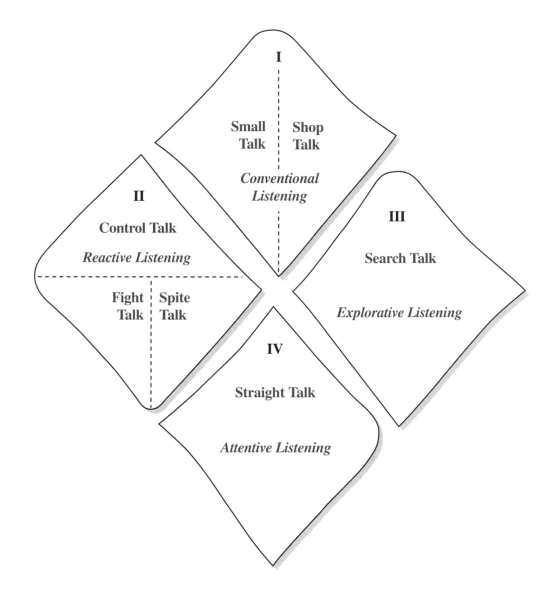

- In the map, each of the talking styles corresponds to a listening style.
- Each style has typical behaviors/skills associated with it that have a predictable impact upon a conversation.

STYLE I

SMALL TALK AND SHOP TALK
CONVENTIONAL LISTENING

Small Talk, Shop Talk, and Conventional Listening represent the sociable styles people use most often to connect and to exchange routine information. The content is ordinary, everyday fare.

SMALL TALK

- This friendly, common, and sometimes playful style helps the world go around. Small Talk maintains the light side of relationships.

- When you want to relax or keep things moving in an easy and comfortable way, you probably use Small Talk. Typically, you intend to be pleasant, find out how the other person is, and not rock the boat.

- This talking style is the way you move in and out of conversations — in person or on the phone — with your family, friends, peers, and strangers. Topics usually involve the weather, news, sports, special events, and other subjects of general interest.

- Small Talk helps build rapport.

Typical Small Talk Behaviors

Hellos and goodbyes: "How are you doing today?" "See you later."

Updating news, weather, sports: "I hear it's supposed to rain today."

Chit chat, passing time: "Who do you think we'll win tomorrow's game?"

Storytelling: "When I was a kid, my Dad would often say . . . ."

Non-hostile joking: "You're not a very good influence on me."

Sharing events of the day: "My biology professor didn't show up today, so I used the time to study for tomorrow's calculus exam."

Discussing biographical data, personal traits, habits, health, appearances: "Where did you grow up?"; "I seldom miss breakfast"; "My shoulder has been sore lately"; "You got a haircut."

Impact of Small Talk

This talking style:

■ Provides relaxing and refreshing time together.

■ Demonstrates basic caring and liking for one another.

■ Lightens a mood with a good joke and a laugh together.

■ Reflects a low or non-existent level of background stress. In a hurried or pressured atmosphere, Small Talk diminishes.

■ Can also be used to cover or avoid dealing with unresolved issues.

SHOP TALK

Shop Talk is essential for carrying on most everyday routine activities. In Shop Talk you focus on task-related matters — maintaining and generating information to get a job done. During an average day, you probably have many Shop-Talk exchanges at work and at home.

Typical Shop Talk Behaviors

Reporting: "The refrigerator is about empty."

Catching up, checking up: "Any calls while I was out?" "Did you feed the pets?"

Providing facts: "The bank closes early on Saturdays."

Scheduling: "How about meeting for lunch tomorrow?"

Following up: "I haven't heard anything more about when the new position will open."

Passing on messages: "There's a message for you on the answering machine."

Impact of Shop Talk

This talking style:

■ Maintains a system.

■ Keeps people informed.

CONVENTIONAL LISTENING

When you want to make contact with others, and be available in a pleasant, sociable way, you listen conventionally.

In Conventional Listening, you:

- Serve as a relaxed sounding board for whatever the speaker offers.
- Show interest in a topic, but expend limited energy.
- Might be involved fully, yet your responses help keep talking on a light level, usually in Small Talk or Shop Talk. At other times, you listen half-heartedly, "with one ear only."

Typical Conventional Listening Behaviors:

Partial attending

Varying eye contact

Casual acknowledgments

Calm body movements

Allowable interruptions

Impact of Conventional Listening

This listening style:

- Shows participation in a relaxing time together.
- Keeps routine matters known.
- Can trigger annoyance or even anger, if someone wants more responsiveness and involvement. (When there are important, non-routine issues to discuss, this listening style is too limited and disengaged to help get to the heart of a matter.)

STYLE I COMMUNICATION

Intention to be:
friendly
sociable
available
playful
pleasant

Intention to:
make contact
build rapport
keep in touch
get along

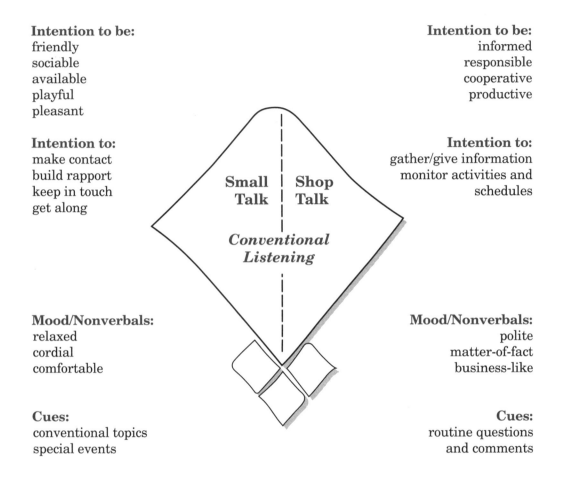

Small Talk | Shop Talk

Conventional Listening

Intention to be:
informed
responsible
cooperative
productive

Intention to:
gather/give information
monitor activities and
schedules

Mood/Nonverbals:
relaxed
cordial
comfortable

Mood/Nonverbals:
polite
matter-of-fact
business-like

Cues:
conventional topics
special events

Cues:
routine questions
and comments

STYLE II

CONTROL TALK, FIGHT TALK, AND SPITE TALK
REACTIVE LISTENING

Style II is a closed style of talking and listening. Its main function is not to generate new information, but rather use power and control to:

- Gain agreement or compliance
- Resist change (yourself)
- Strive for a certain outcome, even if it has to be forced
- Change others (not self)

CONTROL TALK

Control Talk intends to be efficient and constructive. Efforts to take charge and persuade (sell), bargain, supervise, teach, and advocate typically occur in Control Talk.

Typical Control Talk Behaviors

Speaking for others: "That's not what you really want."

Directing: "Just tell her what to do. It's not that hard."

Evaluating: "This new pill is about twice as good as the old one."

Setting expectations, establishing boundaries: "If you're not home tonight by 10 o'clock, don't expect to go out Saturday night."

Advising/prescribing solutions: "You have to take your time with Max. You can't push him. Here's how to handle him . . . ."

Cautioning/warning: "Be careful when you lift that box. The bottom is weak."

Closed/directive/leading questions: "Don't you think that . . . ?" "Wouldn't you agree that . . . ?"

Advocating/selling: "Just try it once. If you don't like it, I won't say anything more."

Assuming/speaking for others: "We'll all be relieved once this is over."

Praising: "The project really came out well. You did a great job!"

Impact of Control Talk

This talking style:

- Takes charge in a proactive, effective, efficient manner.
- Causes others to agree and comply with directives, when it works.
- Can create misunderstanding, distance, and tension, in its brevity and curt efficiency.
- Fosters resistance in others if it is the main style used.
- May generate Fight-or Spite-Talk responses. (Most people like to participate in making decisions that affect them; few people like to be ordered around.)

FIGHT TALK

Fight Talk attempts to force change by attacking others and defending self. It is an aggressive style. Fight Talk:

- Uses active, direct, aggressive, and often punitive language.
- Strives to be in a one-up position of power.
- Focuses on persons rather than the issue.
- *Acts out* fear and anger rather than *acting on* these emotions.
- Avoids/overlooks self's contribution and response to the situation.
- Erupts usually around unclear or disrupted expectations — a change in plans, shortage of time, money, or energy — when people feel fearful, angry, threatened, desperate, or overwhelmed.
- Is reactive, rather than proactive.
- Discounts, devalues others typically.
- Resembles conventional warfare (uses direct, frontal tactics).

Typical Fight Talk Behaviors

Demanding, ordering: "Do it the way I say, and don't ask me why."

Blaming, accusing, attacking, scolding: "Why weren't you paying attention. And don't tell me you were. I saw you with my own eyes."

Threatening consequences, ultimatums: "Do that one more time and that's it!"

Labeling: "You're lazy and irresponsible."

Name-calling, belittling, using loaded words: "Hey stupid, how many times do I have to tell you? That's not the way to do it!"

Defending: "I did it the only way I knew how."

Arguing: "That's not right. It doesn't work that way."

Interrogating: "Tell me what you're thinking. You just sit there with that dumb smile and don't say anything."

Judging/putting down: "If you had a brain, you wouldn't know what to do with it."

Challenging/taunting: "Just try it. You'll fall flat on your face."

Lecturing/moralizing/preaching: "You shouldn't even let those thoughts enter your head."

Bragging: "Ever since I started this job, there hasn't been anyone who could keep up with me."

Psychologizing, diagnosing: "I suggest you find the real cause of your troubles. You're paranoid."

Brutal Confrontation: "You really messed up again. It's obvious you don't have the capability to learn."

Cursing/foul language

Impact of Fight Talk

This talking style:

- Gets juices flowing and may break up a logjam once in awhile.
- Provides ventilation that stirs up, signals an issue.
- Breeds frustration and resentment if used often.
- Creates resistance, pressure, tension and rigidity.
- Interferes with positive long-term solutions to challenging issues.
- Is out of touch with self and other awareness, and consequently out of control.
- Can escalate to physical violence and abuse.
- Often damages relationships — says or does mean and hurtful things that are later regretted.

SPITE TALK

People resort to spiteful messages when they believe they have no other way to influence others and situations. It is a passive-aggressive style. Spite Talk:

- Is indirect and angry, often signaling underlying hurt and resentment.
- Exercises power as *powerlessness* — uses indirect, passive-aggressive non-compliance (resistance).
- May threaten withdrawal, sabotage, or retaliation.
- Exerts control from a one-down, rather than a one-up, position of power.
- Is frequently an indirect expression of helplessness and hopelessness.
- Tries often to spread guilt and shame.
- Tends to discount self or tries to count self in a manipulative way.
- Triangulates issues by talking allusively to an inappropriate third person.
- Resembles guerrilla warfare (uses indirect, hit-and-run tactics).

Typical Spite Talk Behaviors

Shooting zingers, taking pot shots: "If you're so smart, you do it."

Implying poor me — ain't it awful: "Nobody ever asks me if I want to go."

Foot-dragging: "I'll do it when I have time."

Complaining, whining: "How come I always have to do the dirty work?"

Pouting/ignoring: (going about business in silent unresponsiveness)

Withholding information: "I told you once. If you don't remember what I said, I'm not going to repeat it."

Withdrawing angrily: "It's not my problem. Let him hang himself."

Denying: "No, nothing's wrong. What makes you think that?"

Cynicism/sarcasm: "Well, look who claims to have all the answers."

Placating: "No, that's all right. Let's do it your way. I'm sure it will come out better than if we do what I want."

Being a martyr or victim (covering for others, accepting blame): "It was probably my fault again. I should have . . . ."

Putting self down: "If I wasn't so dumb, I would have caught the mistake."

Gossiping/innuendo/being self-righteous: "I never thought she would stoop that low."

Keeping score/getting even: "I won't forget what you just said, and you'll regret it."

Lying/distorting: "I called Pete yesterday (no call was made)."

Attempt to guilt other: "If you were really concerned about me, you would call more often."

Impact of Spite Talk

This talking style:

- Communicates a poor-me attitude.
- Can represent either a long-term lifestyle of low self-esteem or a temporary, wounded response to a particular situation.
- Feeds conflict under the table.
- Drains and diffuses energy.

Tips About Fight and Spite Talk

- Realize that Fight and Spite Talk indicate new or unresolved issues.
- Notice that nonverbals — tone and gestures — signal these styles.
- Recognize these styles as cues to shift to Search or Straight Talk — other more productive styles for dealing with issues.

REACTIVE LISTENING

The intent is to defend or counter a position by listening selectively and trying to deflect or direct the other person's disclosure. Reactive Listening attempts to control or limit information rather than to encourage new and useful information from others.

In this listening style:

- Position replaces understanding.
- The listener listens long enough to formulate a reaction, then interrupts and counters with his or her own perspective.

Typical Reactive Listening Behaviors:

Interrupting to take over the conversation

Disattending to, ignoring critical information

Assuming, mind-reading

Rehearsing internally next statement

Judging constantly, *evaluating, disputing* (whether agreeing or disagreeing)

Asking leading questions that cover the listener's hidden, undisclosed agenda. (For example, "Don't you think . . . ?")

Blaming, calling for justification, often with "why" questions

Crowding (aggressive) or *disengaging* (distancing) gestures

Forcing agreement

Superimposing solutions/actions

Impact of Reactive Listening

This listening style can energize an exchange and even stimulate action. More often however, it is inefficient and generates negative results. Disagreements quickly become power struggles (with players vying for who is right or wrong), rather than information sharing. The result is often an impasse. Lack of listening skills leaves people stuck.

Typically, the style:

- Discounts the talker by attempting to take the floor away from him or her.
- Ignores, twists, distorts, or manipulates what the talker says in an attempt to force agreement or change.
- Increases stress, frustration, and anger.
- Undermines rapport and trust.
- Spawns fragmented, inaccurate, distorted, and misleading information.
- Generates tension, defensiveness, and resistance.
- Prolongs the process of resolution.
- Yields poor decisions.
- Brings long-term loss in quality, time, and money.
- Runs the risk of creating bad feelings and of damaging relationships.
- Creates relationship dissatisfaction.

STYLE II COMMUNICATION

Intention to be:
in charge
helpful
persuasive
efficient

Mood/Nonverbals:
energized
authoritative

Intention to:
control/lead
direct
persuade
instruct
evaluate
set expectations/limits
reinforce positively
use legitimate authority
gain agreement/compliance
ignore

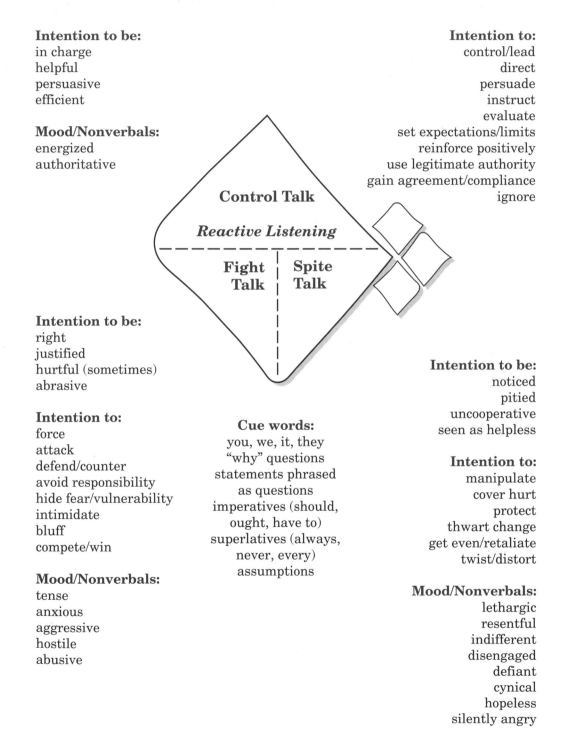

Control Talk

Reactive Listening

Fight Talk   **Spite Talk**

Intention to be:
right
justified
hurtful (sometimes)
abrasive

Intention to:
force
attack
defend/counter
avoid responsibility
hide fear/vulnerability
intimidate
bluff
compete/win

Mood/Nonverbals:
tense
anxious
aggressive
hostile
abusive

Cue words:
you, we, it, they
"why" questions
statements phrased
as questions
imperatives (should,
ought, have to)
superlatives (always,
never, every)
assumptions

Intention to be:
noticed
pitied
uncooperative
seen as helpless

Intention to:
manipulate
cover hurt
protect
thwart change
get even/retaliate
twist/distort

Mood/Nonverbals:
lethargic
resentful
indifferent
disengaged
defiant
cynical
hopeless
silently angry

STYLE III

SEARCH TALK
EXPLORATIVE LISTENING

Search Talk and Explorative Listening revolve around non-routine matters or uncertain and complex issues that may be very fuzzy and undefined. They are cool and rational styles of communication for gaining an overview, exploring facts, and examining possibilities.

SEARCH TALK

Search Talk has a tentative quality to it. You can use it to:

- Speculate about causes
- Brainstorm possibilities
- Pose solutions
- Play out various scenarios without committing yourself to any particular direction

Typical Search Talk Behaviors

Identifying issues: "I'm wondering if I'm having difficulty in making a career choice."

Giving relevant background information: "Last year the tests showed. . ."

Analyzing causes: "Maybe because things came so easy for me so long, I got overconfident."

Giving impressions/explanations: "I think it has to do with how much I exercise. When I'm consistent, I have more energy."

Making interpretations: "Their phone call probably means they're still interested in talking further."

Brainstorming or generating possibilities: "Perhaps I could check into graduate programs in the metro area."

Posing solutions: "I could try this for ninety days, and then make a final decision."

Impact of Search Talk

This talking style:

- Reduces pressure and increases information.
- Becomes a think tank to play out ideas and expand options for the future.
- Is a safe way to test the water by making observations or raising questions.
- Focuses more on past or future time frames than on the present.
- Skims across the surface often and misses the core of an issue.
- Can be a sophisticated way to avoid resolving issues — where no one takes responsibility for putting ideas into action.
- Can leave you and others dissatisfied from lack of closure.

EXPLORATIVE LISTENING

Open questions dominate the Explorative Listening style. They are used to search for significant information surrounding complex or non-routine issues.

In this style, open questions:

- Guide the conversation
- Probe for information in a non-accusatory fashion
- Are intended to:

  Gain perspective

  Expand knowledge

  Clarify misunderstandings

  Clear up confusion

Explorative Listening Behaviors

Asking open questions, the listening skill used primarily in Explorative Listening, is presented in detail in Chapter 6, page 83.

Impact of Explorative Listening

This listening style:

- Increases attending.
- Takes the pressure off the moment by opening the discussion.
- Generates possibilities.
- Can intentionally or unintentionally limit an exchange.
- Increases the quality of information over Conventional or Reactive styles of listening.

Search Talk and Exploratory Listening work best in combination with the next talking and listening styles, Straight Talk and Attentive Listening, to get to the heart of issues and take action.

STYLE III COMMUNICATION

Intention to be:
rational
expansive
flexible
insightful
safe

Mood/Nonverbals:
calm
tentative
inquisitive
supportive
intellectual

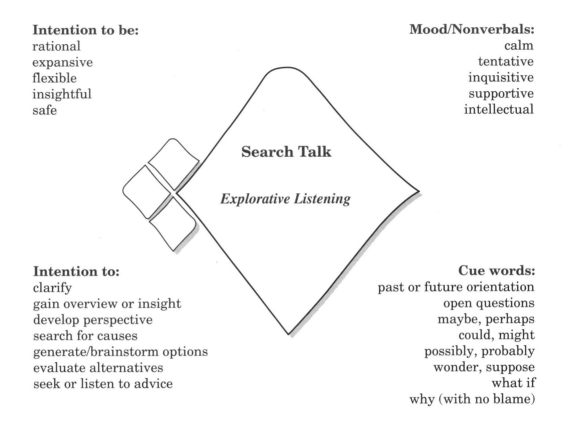

Search Talk

Explorative Listening

Intention to:
clarify
gain overview or insight
develop perspective
search for causes
generate/brainstorm options
evaluate alternatives
seek or listen to advice

Cue words:
past or future orientation
open questions
maybe, perhaps
could, might
possibly, probably
wonder, suppose
what if
why (with no blame)

STYLE IV

STRAIGHT TALK
ATTENTIVE LISTENING

Straight Talk and Attentive Listening go to the heart of an issue. The communication discloses self-information, particularly parts left unsaid in other styles — typically feelings and wants. Likewise, the style tunes into others, to understand a situation as the others do.

STRAIGHT TALK

In Straight Talk, you:

- *Focus* on your own experience — self-awareness in the present, now.

- *Accept* what you find as *what is*, rather than disregard, deny, or run from it.

- *Own* your own *contributions* and *responses* to an issue or situation.

- *Act on,* not react to, this awareness.

In conversation, you use all the talking skills presented in Chapter II, pages 59-62 to:

- Disclose all parts of your Awareness Wheel, including significant feelings and wants.

- Deal *completely* and *congruently* with tension, differences, and conflict without blaming, demanding, defending, or deceiving.

- Channel your energy into positive change.

- Work through issues and resolve personal and interpersonal conflicts peacefully — generating collaborative outcomes when possible.

Typical Straight Talk Behaviors

Dealing with the issue: "Here's how I see what's going on."

Identifying tension: "I'm feeling very frustrated right now."

Acknowledging differences: "Well, I think we're at opposite poles on this point."

Requesting feedback: "Do I do something that shuts you off, after you begin to talk?"

Giving feedback: "I've noticed that sometimes you drop your voice at the end of a sentence. When this happens, I think you don't have confidence in what you are saying."

Expressing appreciation: "Thank you for your encouragement. Your support gives me confidence to move ahead on this tough decision."

Revealing impact/sharing vulnerability: "Going back to school really scares me. I don't think I've got what it takes to hang in there."

Taking responsibility for your own contribution/response: "When you make a suggestion, I often shoot it down without really hearing what it is you are saying."

Asking for change: "The joke about socks isn't funny for me anymore. I don't want to hear it again. Will you agree to stop saying it?"

Apologizing: "I think I really offended you by not getting your input. I'm sorry I did that and want to assure you that I will not do that again."

Giving support: "I will back up your decision."

Impact of Straight Talk

This talking style:

- Helps you discuss a difficult matter if your intentions are to connect and collaborate rather than to control and manipulate.

- Gains its real power from putting your cards/agenda on the table without playing tricks.

- Results in more helpful information and richer interchange.

- Lets you be recognized as an authority on your own experience.

- Builds trust as you share your real thoughts, feelings, and wants about issues.

- Has its limits. It is not a "cure all" or "quick fix." It does not guarantee you will get what you want. It demonstrates commitment to an open process.

Straight Talk Brings Risk and Opportunity

- As you disclose more about yourself, you increase the listeners' choices — what they can do constructively or destructively about the information you supply.

- Usually disclosure begets disclosure and results in new understanding, satisfaction, and productivity.

ATTENTIVE LISTENING

One of the quickest ways to connect with someone about an issue is to listen attentively to him or her — letting that person express his or her awareness — wherever that leads you.

Attentive Listening Skills:

Attentive Listening revolves primarily around four of the five listening skills in the Listening Cycle described in Chapter 6, pages 87-96. They include:

> Attending — looking, listening, tracking
>
> Acknowledging the other's experience
>
> Inviting more information
>
> Summarizing to ensure accuracy

(The skill of asking open questions typically occurs with Explorative Listening, Style III communication.)

In the Attentive Listening style, you:

- Put your concerns aside temporarily.
- Simply follow what the other is saying.
- Do not rehearse, evaluate, or redirect.
- Let yourself be in the other person's shoes.

Impact of Attentive Listening

This listening style:

- Reduces interpersonal tension, establishes rapport, and builds trust.
- Creates the most complete and accurate information base.
- Enhances the esteem of the players in the process.
- Earns the right to be heard.

STYLE IV COMMUNICATION

Intention to be:
open
clear
direct
truthful/accurate
responsible/accountable
present
engaging
responsive
respectful
tactful

Intention to:
care
disclose
understand
attune/follow
act on "what is"
connect, not control
count self and other
collaborate

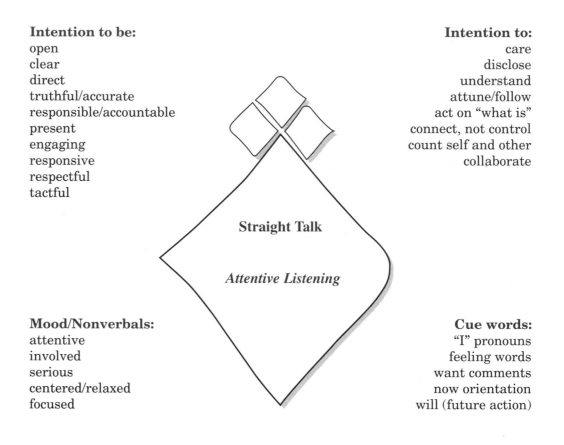

Straight Talk

Attentive Listening

Mood/Nonverbals:
attentive
involved
serious
centered/relaxed
focused

Cue words:
"I" pronouns
feeling words
want comments
now orientation
will (future action)

PRACTICAL USES OF STYLES

- People negotiate how they relate through styles, that is, work out the rapport, control, trust, and amount of information they share. Being aware of styles can help you understand and change the nature of your relationships.

- Knowing the communication styles increases your choices in how to deal with issues, which is particularly important when you are under pressure or when a conflict arises.

- No one style is best, and no style handles all situations. Each style has a function. The key is to *match style and situation appropriately,* so you avoid getting stuck in a counterproductive style.

- Styles provide a practical framework for diagnosis and intervention — for *assessing* ineffective communication patterns and for *facilitating* change.

GENERALIZATIONS ABOUT STYLES
(EMPHASIS ON STYLES II AND IV)

- Generally, you get the style that you give. Style II gets Style II in response. Usually Style IV gets Style IV in response.

- Style II tries to control others by limiting information. Style IV tries to connect with others by expanding information.

- Style II tries to exert power over others. Style IV demonstrates power over self.

- Do not confuse Straight Talk with a brutal confrontation (Fight Talk). This usually begins, "Let me be straight with you," and then proceeds to attack in Fight Talk.

- Fight and Spite (tension) signal new or unresolved issues. A buildup of Fight and Spite Talk usually indicates a troubled, unhappy relationship-system.

- The combined use of Styles III and IV support an *open process* for real relationship-system change. They enable you to use your experience to learn and grow.

This book offers skills and processes to help you improve your use of the styles Straight Talk, Explorative Listening, and Attentive Listening.

EXERCISE: WHAT ARE MY STYLES?

Instructions

Step 1. Think of the styles of communication you use during a day. Estimate the percent of time you *typically* spend in each style, talking and listening. Then give a percent for your *desired* usage.

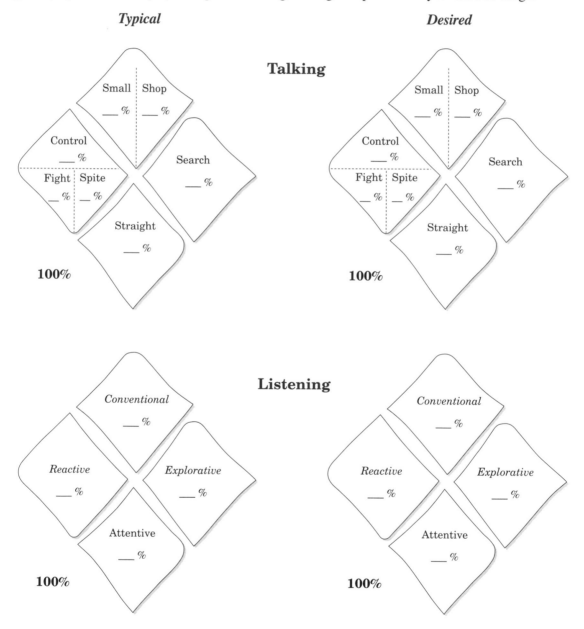

Step 2. Choose styles for yourself to increase (circle them) and decrease (cross them off).

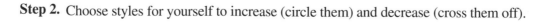

SECTION II

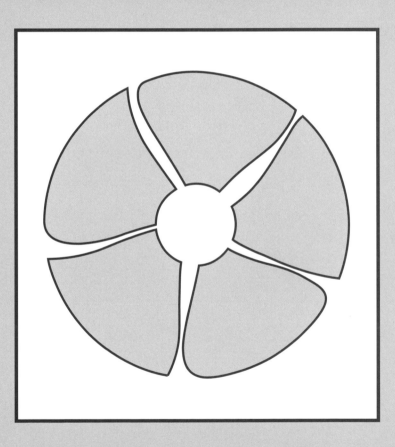

2

INTERACTIVE PRINCIPLES

SOS Systems
Caring and Communication
Issues

SOS SYSTEMS

Principle: Issues affect parts and whole.

We operate in relationship networks — small sub-systems of family, friends, neighbors, and associates at work, school, and elsewhere. When issues arise, most often they involve other people in some way. SOS helps you think systemically, considering all the people that an issue involves or affects.

S	O	S
Self	**Other(s)**	**Stakeholders**
Yourself	People who are *immediately/ centrally* involved	People who are *peripherally* involved yet still affected

Like a ripple effect in water, a change that an issue brings in one person or part of a system affects the other people, too, the whole relationship system — SOS.

CARING AND COMMUNICATION

Principle: Your behavior and attitude reflect one another.

Every message you communicate contains two parts:

> **Behavior** — Observable words and actions.
>
> **Attitude** — Underlying beliefs, feelings, and intentions.

Behavior

Your words and actions — your verbal or non-verbal behaviors that other people observe — influence:

- how you come across to others
- how they respond to you

Your behavior — actions and reactions — create exchanges with others. These experiences in turn stimulate or modify your own attitudes and those you influence in others.

Attitudes

Attitudes express your momentary or long-term assumptions about your own or someone else's significance. You can hold one of these two attitudes:

- I don't care about (count, value, consider). . .

- I care about (count, value, consider). . .

Attitude is a Choice

The choice is always yours to communicate, either "I don't care . . ." or "I care . . ."

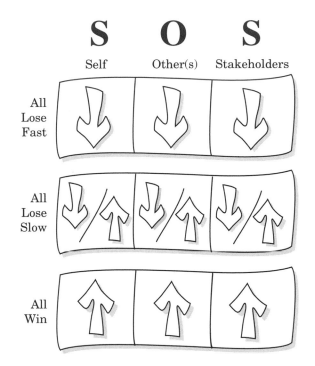

Consider these points:

■ People are often interconnected and interdependent.

■ Each person is a resource that can be counted or discounted.

■ Differences between and among the people in the SOS System increase the potential for conflict.

■ Poor solutions discount someone in the SOS System.

■ Counting SOS, while sometimes difficult and complicated, is essential for creating best-fit solutions for challenging issues.

Skill and Caring (Behavior and Attitude)

Skilled or unskilled communication behaviors in combination with an uncaring or caring attitude bring certain kinds of outcomes. They also influence personal esteem and relationship development.

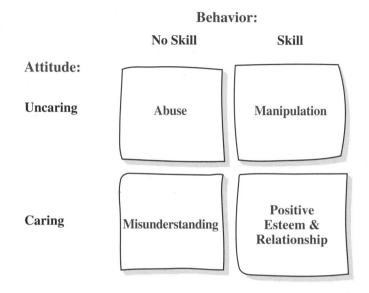

- Lack of skill and an uncaring attitude — either toward self or another — produce abusive situations. These can extend from verbal or psychological abuse all the way to physical abuse.

- Skilled behavior with an uncaring attitude can permit you to manipulate or take advantage of another, particularly if the other is less skilled.

- Lack of skill and a caring attitude leave room for misunderstanding and unclear or inept communication.

- Skilled behavior and a caring attitude help you resolve issues effectively while you develop good self- and other-esteem in your exchanges; plus they help you strengthen your relationships.

Skills are Learnable

When you combine the skills with a caring attitude toward yourself, others, and stakeholders, you can work out the issues of your life more satisfactorily.

EXERCISE: CARING COUNTS

One way to understand an important issue/situation is to think about who is being counted and discounted.

Instructions: Think about several specific events or decisions involving yourself and other(s) over the past several months. For each issue/situation consider which people in the SOS System were counted or discounted:

Issue/Situation	SOS	How Counted/Discounted	Outcome

Issue/Situation	SOS	How Counted/Discounted	Outcome

Issue/Situation	SOS	How Counted/Discounted	Outcome

THE CONTENT OF ISSUES

Principle: Issues indicate something is changing or must change.

Often people want to communicate better so they can deal more effectively with the issues that arise in the course of daily living, particularly when the issues bring conflict.

An issue is anything (situation, event, experience, awareness, opportunity) that concerns you or any other person in your SOS network and requires resolution. Issues grow out of a gap between what is *anticipated or desired* and what is *experienced,* between what *could be* or *should be* and *what is not.*

The Content Focus of Issues

Recall from the Introduction that three forces drive issues — the *content,* the *outcome,* and the *process* used in dealing with them. Consider first the content of an issue or "what it is all about" — the information concerning it.

Issues tend to have a primary type of content focus, which falls into one of four categories:

- Topical — places, things, tasks and technical matters
- Personal — self, *or* other, *or* stakeholder as an individual
- Relational — interaction between people, typically between self and other(s), between other(s) and other(s), or between other(s) and stakeholder(s)
- Group — an organizational unit — family, work or leisure team, committee, or department

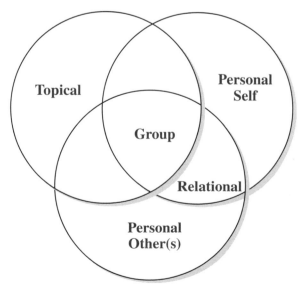

Issues may have a primary focus (topical, personal, relational or group), or be composed of a combination of content types.

TYPES OF ISSUES

Topical

Children	Friends	Projects
Chores	Housing	Relatives
Clothes	Leisure	Space
Drugs/alcohol	Money	Sports
Education	Moving	Time
Exercise	Parents	Travel
Food	Pets	Work

Personal — Self *or* Other *or* Stakeholder

Appearance	Failure	Productivity
Attitude	Faith	Recognition
Career	Freedom	Responsibility
Creativity	Goals	Self-esteem
Death	Habits	Skills
Discipline	Health	Success
Energy	Identity	Values

Relational — Self and Other(s)

Closeness/distance	Acceptance
Collaboration/competition	Affection
Conflict/harmony	Appreciation
Equality/subordination	Boundaries
Inclusion/exclusion	Commitment
Similarity/difference	Communication
Stability/change	Fun
Support/control	Sex
Togetherness/apartness	Trust

Group — as Unit

Esprit de corps
Feedback
Participation
Productivity
Purpose
Resources/constraints
Stage of development
Structure/leadership

Points About the Content of Issues

- Any content focus can be viewed as positive or negative.

- Issues tend to get "riskier" and more intense as the focus moves from topical to relational.

- Dealing with issues of differing content types requires varying amounts of mental and emotional energy as well as material resources.

- Knowing the differences among the types of content focus can help you identify and deal with your issues more clearly.

EXERCISE: INVENTORY OF YOUR CURRENT ISSUES

Date: _____

Instructions: Take a few minutes, relax, and think about what is going on in your life at the present time. Think about your activities at home, work, school, and elsewhere. As you reflect, write down a word or phrase that represents the topical, personal, or relational concerns that come to your mind. (If something is too personal for this setting, you may choose not to write it down.)

Issues

3

THE AWARENESS WHEEL MAP

Self Talk
Talking Skills

THE MAP OF AN ISSUE

All issues, regardless of content focus, have an underlying structure. They are made up of five types of information. Similar to the way a simple sentence contains basic parts — subject, verb, and object, your experience of an issue contains basic parts — sensory data, thoughts, feelings, wants, and actions. The Awareness Wheel presents this structure.

Each part of the Awareness Wheel contains important information. Parts are distinct yet interact with one another. They are present whether or not you are conscious of them, and they become useful to you once you are aware of them.

THE AWARENESS WHEEL — A USEFUL TOOL

The Awareness Wheel, a map of experience, provides an information guide to help you work through any issue you face. As a tool, the Awareness Wheel map:

■ Brings clarity and organizes the five parts for you.

■ Helps you to understand yourself and others better in relation to an issue.

■ Helps you resolve issues more efficiently, less stressfully.

■ Supports better decisions and gives you more confidence in your decisions, because you know you have considered all the parts.

■ Is particularly valuable when conflict is involved.

Benefits of Awareness

Your awareness of the parts of the Wheel influences the process you use to deal with an issue, and often determines its outcome. Consider these points:

■ Self awareness informs and facilitates your decisions.

■ Expanding awareness increases your choices in how you interact with others and allows you to communicate better.

■ On the other hand, if you are less aware or unaware you:

Make poor decisions.

Send partial or confusing (sometimes frustrating) messages.

Are easily misunderstood by others.

Do not realize how you impact others.

■ Awareness is foundational for putting the talking and listening skills to work in dealing effectively with conflicts that issues can bring.

■ Even when conflict does not exist, when you simply want to reflect on something, make a decision, or share an experience with another, awareness helps you do so more satisfactorily.

■ Self awareness increases self control.

The Awareness Wheel details the parts of your experience in five zones, as follows.

SENSATIONS — Your Sensory Data

Sensory Data — sight, sound, smell, taste, and touch — are inputs to you.

External Data

You gather data from other people as:

facial expressions	movement	scent	words
gestures	posture	tones	

The verbal and nonverbal behaviors of other people — what you hear them say and see them do— are sensory input from a source external to you. Their closeness or distance, energy level, and words all become part of your sensory database. Your senses constantly scan your environment to pick up data from people and other things.

Other external data include:

- Context — time, place, sound, and others present
- Output from equipment, and printed material (including media)

Your five senses provide you with immediate and past (recalled) contact with your world. Observation allows you to document your perceptions. Realize that the more you pay attention to the subtleties, as well as the obvious aspects, of what you see, hear, smell, taste, and touch, the more you will be aware of the part of your experience that comes from outside.

Internal Data

Bodily Sensations

Sensory data also come to your awareness from inside your own body — for example, physical pain, goose bumps, fatigue, hunger, a chill, or fever.

Intuitive Sensations

These data come from your internal world of memories, associations, dreams, and so forth. When an intuitive sensation occurs, you may find it difficult to document your perceptions with sensory data, partly because intuitive sensations often draw on bits or fragments of both external and internal data. Sometimes a small piece of sensory data from the external world triggers the intuitive sensation. When you explore the source of the sensation, however, it is usually possible to describe the specific external and internal data.

THOUGHTS — The Meaning You Make

Thoughts are the meanings you make out of the sensory data you receive.

Three basic forms of thoughts correspond generally with your past, present, and future thinking:

- *Beliefs* — your collected experience from the past, which you bring to each new situation. Beliefs are powerful and can limit or expand what can grow out of an experience.

- *Interpretations* — the meaning you make currently of sensory data. This includes the logical, analytical, and rational processes of weighing data to arrive at a conclusion. Interpretations represent the way you put your world together — your operating hypothesis.

- *Expectations* — the future you anticipate — what you think will happen — based on what you have seen, heard, or perceived from some other sensory data.

Other words that signal thinking processes include:

assumptions	guesses	judgments	opinions
benefits	reasons	metaphors	predictions
conclusions	ideas	needs	principles
evaluations	impressions	objections	values

Points to Consider:

- Sometimes thoughts can be quite illogical or inconsistent with evidence.

- It is possible to create, imagine, or select pieces of sensory data to fit your beliefs, interpretations, and expectations. This can result in bias and distortion.

- Others may see and hear the same data and come to very different conclusions.

- Your beliefs, interpretations, and expectations are very powerful forces. They are strong influences on your decisions and actions.

- In addition to sensory data, other parts of the Awareness Wheel interact with your thoughts.

FEELINGS — Your Emotions

Feelings, or emotions, are your spontaneous physiological responses to your interpretation of sensory data. They are biological reactions that happen within you, and they register in your body.

Six Basic Feelings

Each of these six basic emotions creates a different set of physiological effects:

happiness, sadness, anger, fear, disgust, and surprise

Changes in heart rate, blood flow, and hormonal activity occur in your body, depending on the emotion.

You experience variations of the basic emotions and others, as well. For example, you can feel:

annoyed	disappointed	frustrated	peaceful
anxious	distressed	glad	pleased
ashamed	eager	guilty	proud
calm	embarrassed	hurt	relieved
cautious	elated	irritated	satisfied
contented	enthusiastic	jealous	scared
comfortable	excited	joyful	terrified
delighted	frightened	lonely	uneasy

What About Feelings?

Feelings do not just come out of the blue. Instead, as you make meaning of the sensory data in a situation, positive or negative emotions occur. For example, the data may or may not match your beliefs, expectations, or desires at the time. The stronger your beliefs, expectations, or desires, the stronger the resulting feelings.

As you take in sensory data, interpret it, and respond emotionally, all of this happens instantaneously, without your bidding; thus, you are passive to the emotions you experience. Because emotions reflect your interpretation of what is going on in the other parts of your Awareness Wheel, feelings are quite rational and predictable. This is why you can learn to trust your emotions as useable information.

Your body gives clues or signals to your feelings. If you tune into your own body you can often locate where you feel your emotions. For example, you may recognize a certain sensation in your stomach when you are excited or afraid. Anger shows in the tightening of upper body muscles and flushed skin. Muscles are more relaxed with the feeling of happiness.

Points to Consider:

■ If your emotions are not distorted by drugs (sometimes including prescription drugs), alcohol, organic disease, or untoward learning about emotions, feelings function like a gauge. They give you a reliable reading — positive to negative, and strong to weak — of a situation.

■ Like an alarm, feelings can signal new or unresolved issues — that something has changed or needs attention in another zone of your Wheel.

■ Emotions help you judge your level of satisfaction with the process and the outcome of an issue.

■ Since feelings are part of what is, they do not have to be justified, denied, or avoided. If you do not attend to your emotions, you miss important self information that is essential for making good decisions or resolving conflicts.

■ Emotions are universal to the human experience; however, some emotions, such as guilt and shame, are culturally generated.

■ Even though your emotions occur without your immediate control, once you gain awareness of them, they lose power over you. Also, as you recognize and acknowledge them, you can learn ways to manage yourself and express them appropriately.

Thoughts are Often Confused with Feelings

While using the word *feel* for *think* (e.g. I feel that . . .) is common in our language, this use does not differentiate adequately your thoughts from your emotions. The two kinds of information are qualitatively distinct. Confusing the two limits the clarity of your awareness and communication.

Two examples of the confusion include:
> "I feel *rejected.*"
> "I feel *threatened:*"

These are thoughts. Notice what happens when you understand *rejected* and *threatened* as thoughts, and not emotions. It puts you actively in charge of your thinking, and aware of your associated feelings. For example:

> "I think I'm being rejected. I feel hurt and sad."

> "I believe I'm being threatened. I feel scared and angry."

When an issue is involved, most thoughts have one or more feelings associated with them. Thoughts that typically produce considerable affect (emotion) are easy to confuse with feelings. For increased awareness and clearer communication, keep the two straight.

> Here is a partial list of some thought words that are commonly expressed as emotions. As you read over the list, identify the emotions (sometimes strong emotions) that often accompany these thoughts:
>
> | | | |
> |---|---|---|
> | Abandoned | Dominated | Righteous |
> | Betrayed | Important | Slighted |
> | Challenged | Insulted | Tempted |
> | Cheated | Persecuted | Threatened |
> | Childish | Pressured | Thwarted |
> | Conspicuous | Rejected | Unloved |
> | Deceitful | Respected | Adequate/inadequate |
> | Defeated | Rewarded | Competent/incompetent |

WANTS — Your Desires

The zone of wants in the Awareness Wheel refers to your desires for yourself and for others, short-term or long-term and general or specific.

Common words associated with wants include:

aspirations	goals	longings	targets
dreams	hopes	motives	wishes
drives	intentions	objectives	yearnings

Three types of wants, with examples, include:

- *To be*: healthy, honest, respected, appreciated, liked, successful,
- *To do* — general or specific

   General: compete, collaborate, get even, clarify, support

   Specific: finish a project, change jobs, go out to dinner

- *To have*: ticket to a special concert, a different car, good friends

Wants are an inclination to act and imply a movement towards or away from something or someone. They motivate and energize you. They vary in intensity from weak to strong (as do the resulting feelings when sensory data show they are achieved or not).

Sometimes wants start as a vague dream or fantasy and then turn into specific objectives. They remain tentative, as intentions to act, until they are translated into future actions or next steps. By themselves, wants do not change things.

Points About Wants

- You can have multiple wants, and they can either blend together or compete with one another.

- When your wants are fragmented or conflicting, they can scatter your energy and lead to incongruent behavior.

- Hidden wants (perhaps because they are not acceptable to yourself or others important to you) become hidden agenda. They result in confusing, misleading, or dishonest communication.

- Clarifying and prioritizing your wants can help focus your energy.

CARING ABOUT:

S	O	S
Self	**Other(s)**	**Stakeholders**
Yourself	People who are *immediately/ centrally* involved	People who are *peripherally* involved yet still affected

Wants *For* Versus *From*

When we attend to wants, we often first think of self: my interests, what I desire *for* myself. This shows caring about self and is important to recognize. When it comes to thinking about others, it easy to think only about what I want *from* others (*for* self) — not *for* others and their interests.

Wants For Others and Stakeholders Builds Bridges

Wants *for* other(s) means that I attend to and acknowledge others' interests — what I have heard them say they want. Wants *for* others means to the extent possible, I want for them what they want; I support them in fulfilling their interests when possible. This demonstrates caring about others and stakeholders.

The difference between *from* others and *for* others is significant, and requires real understanding of another and the ability to put yourself in that person's shoes (discover some of his or her Awareness Wheel).

The Big Test

The big test is whether the others agree that *your wants for them* match *what they want for themselves* — based on what they have actually said they want.

■ Caution: It is easy to want *for* others what you think would be good for them (what they *should* want). This does not pass the test.

■ If you really do not care about the others, you will not be concerned about their wants.

Tips

■ When you can connect with others' wants and help them achieve their objectives, you strengthen the relationship.

■ If you cannot affirm all the wants, at least acknowledge them and look for wants you can affirm. Usually, some point exists around which you can connect and build.

■ If you do not know what others really want, ask them. Get data about their wants.

■ A relationship or system that cannot or does not attend to and support each person's interests, when possible, is a relationship or system in some degree of trouble. This is diagnostic.

■ Look for others' wants that you can support, with no strings attached, as a gift to them.

Wants Are a Critical Part of Solutions

■ When you use your Awareness Wheel, you actively identify your wants *for* SOS — the whole system. This information supports the process of creating best-fit solutions — the most satisfying outcomes for everyone involved.

■ Considering wants *for* SOS is critical for individual, pair, or group solutions.

■ The difference between *from* others and *for* others provides a potential connecting point — the foundation for collaboration — especially in negotiating, decision-making, and conflict-resolving situations.

■ While not always easy, affirming wants for SOS is essential for effective systems thinking and change.

What you want comes out *directly* or *indirectly* (as hidden agenda) in your actions, the next part of the Awareness Wheel.

ACTIONS — Your Behavior

This zone of the Awareness Wheel refers to what you say and do — your verbal and nonverbal behaviors — past, present, and future. Actions result from how you process sensory data, thoughts, feelings, and wants.

Actions include your:

activities	contracts	promises
agreements	nonverbal:	questions
commands	sounds, gestures, motions	statements
commitments		words

Time is an important factor:

- Past Action: what you have said or have done earlier (yesterday, last week, last year, or before).

- Present Action: what you say or do currently.

- Future Action: what you *will* do at a specific point in time (next hour, tomorrow, or next week). Thus, future actions put your *will* into motion and include a commitment to act.

Note that in this zone, actions are your own words and behaviors and not those of someone else.

Points to Consider

- Your actions (output) are the sensory data (input) for others.
- Your actions demonstrate your choices.

Notes About Future Actions

- It may be helpful in dealing with an issue to think of future actions as small next steps.
- Not every issue requires that you choose a future action immediately (you may need additional time to reflect), or sometimes even at all. For a certain issue, just being aware of other parts of your experience (all the other parts of the Wheel) may be enough to help you understand and settle it for you.
- Consider whether your not taking a future action will keep you stuck unnecessarily on an issue.

ISSUES AND THE AWARENESS WHEEL

Issues arise when an *external* or *internal* signal/alarm goes off. The cue can come from any zone of your Wheel:

- Unexpected or surprising *sensory data*
- Unclear, confusing, or disturbing *thoughts*
- Uncomfortable *feelings*
- Unfulfilled or conflicting *wants*
- Inappropriate or ineffective *actions* or *inaction*

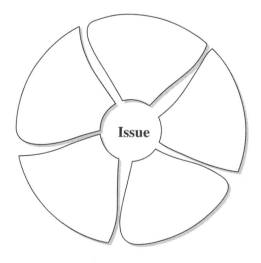

SELF-TALK: USING YOUR AWARENESS WHEEL

Self-talk is the intrapersonal process of connecting with all parts of yourself in order to resolve an issue.

Use the Awareness Wheel as a Tool to Self-Talk Your Way Through the Issue.

- Privately ask yourself, "What's going on right now? What am I experiencing?"

- Expand your awareness and organize the chaos to analyze the issue.

- Cover all parts of the Wheel in any order — all parts of your Wheel are interrelated.

- Be honest with yourself. Accept what you find as where you are — the starting point for dealing with the issue.

- Fill in blind spots (missing self-information).

- Keep processing the issue until something shifts in your awareness and all parts come together, so you can choose a constructive next step (future action) that fits congruently. (Remember, future action can be a small next step.)

The 80/20 rule says important information is inside yourself — use it.

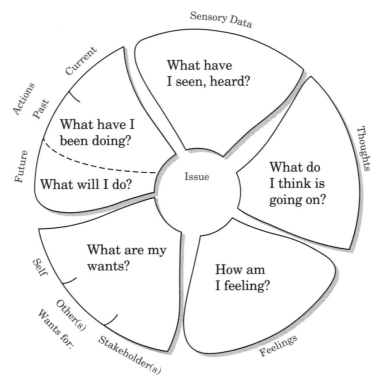

Points to Consider

- If an obvious next step (future action) does not emerge immediately, go around the Wheel again — take a deep breath, let yourself relax, and re-cycle the issue. Like peeling an onion, this allows your deeper, less obvious (conscious) thoughts, feelings, and wants to emerge.

- In the process of systematically examining an issue occasionally, you will discover opposing information or parts that do not fit together comfortably (for example, a want that does not square with a thought or feeling). The Wheel guides you to the points of internal conflict you must resolve in the process of choosing an effective future action — the next step.

- If a clear next step or new awareness does not emerge after recycling the Wheel a couple of times, set the issue (your Wheel) aside for a while. Go on living, letting your current awareness interact ("cook") with new data and emerging experience. In the meanwhile, you can be confident that you have a tool to help you manage yourself and the issue as it unfolds.

- Do not expect the process of Self-Talk always to be completed at one time. Often it takes days or much longer to work through an issue — depending on its complexity and importance. In these instances, use Self-Talk to "huddle with yourself" occasionally for a process check along the way, until an outcome emerges.

- Note that you can experience the negative form of zones of the Wheel: "I did not see . . . "; "I don't think . . . "; "I'm not happy . . . "; "I do not want . . . "; "I did not do . . . ."

- Sometimes the issue you start with is not the real issue. Rather, in the process of expanding your awareness, you discover a deeper, more central or encompassing concern to be the major concern.

- Using the Wheel for Self-Talk can be a very useful and powerful experience. Other times it is non-eventful. It often depends on your readiness at the time.

- Not all issues are easily resolved with Self-Talk. Sometimes you must involve other people, too. What the process does do is heighten your awareness of your choices, including a difficult one. It is a start.

SELF-TALK EXERCISE

Instructions

Choose an issue — topical, personal, or relational — that you would be willing to share in a small group with three other people. (Refer to your list of issues on page 40.)

Write the issue in the hub of the Awareness Wheel below. Then, fill out your Wheel, in any order, using key words or phrases that represent your experience regarding the issue.

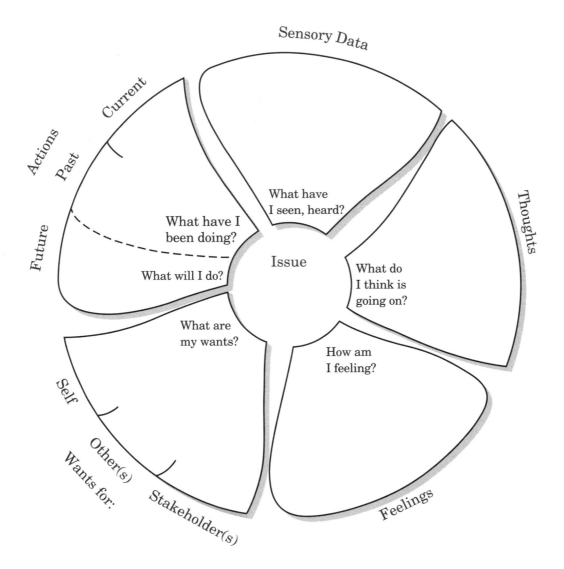

HOW TO USE —
THE AWARENESS WHEEL SKILLS MAT

Skills mats are tools to help you learn communication skills faster and better. They combine left and right brain activity to prompt, organize, and express awareness. They aid you in practicing the skills and coaching someone else on them.

The Awareness Wheel mat helps you to access deeper, clearer, and more complete information about yourself. You do this by physically stepping from zone to zone on the mat.

To Use the Awareness Wheel Skills Floor Mat

- Place the mat on the floor so you can step on it. Be sure the mat does not slip on the floor when you step on it. Set the mat so that you can read the words (facing you) as you look down.

- Start by standing on "Issue" at the center, briefly identifying the issue.

- Move to whatever zone you are experiencing as you speak your thoughts, feelings, wants, and so on. Let yourself fully experience that zone.

- Let your awareness be your guide to where to step, or use the zones on the mat to prompt your awareness (fill in information) when you are not sure of what you are experiencing in a particular zone or part of a zone.

- Move crisscross or in any direction (sometimes rather quickly), to represent the different fragments of awareness as they come to you. Be sure your reflections accurately correspond with the zone on which you are stepping. (For example, move to "thoughts" when you think thoughts and to "feelings" when you feel emotions.)

- Continue to move from zone to zone until your awareness is complete or you are ready to stop.

- Call **Time Out** at any point and step off the mat. (Perhaps your emotions run too high, you feel overwhelmed or saturated with so much information, or you need more time away to reflect.)

- Step to **Check Process** at any point by saying, "I want to check the process." And then continue by asking, for example, "Am I aligned accurately in this zone of the Wheel?" or "Is it someone else's turn to talk?" or " Am I hearing a solution?"

When it becomes clear from Self-Talk that your next step is to talk with a particular person about the issue, use the talking skills, which the next section shows you how to do.

HOW TO OBSERVE AND COACH —
USING THE AWARENESS WHEEL SKILLS MAT

When you are the observer-coach for someone who is moving about the Awareness Wheel mat, sharing his or her awareness:

- Look for accuracy.

- Notice if statements match zones. Examples of mismatches include:

    — Feel instead of think — "I feel that . . ."

    — Want from other, instead of a clear want for other

    — Action (my behavior) versus sensory data (observations of others' actions)

- Notice if all zones of the Awareness Wheel are covered (or any are missed).

To Coach:

- Prior to a person beginning his or her story on the mat, ask whether he or she wants coaching during the exercise. If so, coach. If not, do not coach.

- Focus on process.

    — Coach *process* — about the zones of the Awareness Wheel rather than about *content* or *outcome* (solutions).

- For a mismatch:

    — Simply point with your foot, aligning the talker with the zone he or she is expressing.

- For missing information:

    — Wait until the person has completed the story; then say, for instance, "I noticed that you did not mention your feelings. Do you wish to fill in that zone?"

    — If a person misses the future action, point it out, but do not pressure him or her to take any specific action. Sometimes a person just tries to understand an issue; future action commitment comes later.

Coaching Tips

- Let each person tell his or her own story, in the sequence and at the pace the individual chooses.

- Make coaching brief and specific, so the storyteller does not lose momentum.

- Be careful not to over-direct — especially with questions.

- Give positive feedback about parts a person does well.

TALKING SKILLS — STRAIGHT TALK, STYLE IV

If you decide to share your self-information, based on the Awareness Wheel, with someone else, six talking skills will help you do so more clearly, directly, and completely. The six skills are:

1. SPEAK FOR SELF

This skill is basic to all the other talking skills. It is critical to making your message more apt to be listened to and accepted rather than ignored and rejected.

To speak for yourself, combine a personal pronoun — I, me, my, or mine — with any part(s) of your Awareness Wheel to form a message.

> "I saw you hesitate and then talk."
>
> "Here's my idea."
>
> "Your response really pleases me."
>
> "I'd like more time to think about it."
>
> "I'll call you Thursday."

Speaking for Self — a Signal for High Self Esteem:

- Uniqueness — my individuality, in diversity
- Ownership — my responsibility and accountability
- Confidence— the legitimacy and validity of my own self
- Authority — my acknowledgement and acceptance of my experience
- Assertion — the right to speak my own awareness

Other Benefits of Speaking for Self:

- Makes messages clearer and easier to hear
- Reduces defensiveness/resistance in others
- Leaves room for others' views — differences
- Values self, respects others

An Ineffective Process Often Develops When You Speak for Other(s) or No One

Over-Responsible	Self-Responsible	Under-Responsible
Speaks for Other(s) (in 2nd person)	**Speaks for Self** (in 1st person)	**Speaks for No One** (in 3rd person)
You, We, Everyone Statements	I, Me, My, Mine Statements	It, One, Some People Statements

Speaking for Others

To speak for others involves making "you," "we," or "every-one" statements. People who do this:

- Superimpose their views on others
- Are often invasive, intrusive
- Generate defensiveness and resistance (simply by the way they say it)
- Attempt to fence other(s) in
- Deny difference, uniqueness
- Discount others

"You shouldn't feel that way."

"We don't believe that."

"Everyone knows better."

Speaking For No One

People who speak for no one talk indirectly, cautiously, and in uncommitted ways. They lack authority, and others soon devalue their opinions, intentions, and feelings, too. They also:

- Fear ownership
- Lack confidence
- Avoid clarity and directness (about who is talking or what is meant)
- Seem distant, often cold
- Discount self

"It might be good to consider this."

"One could get upset about this."

"Some people don't care."

2. DESCRIBE SENSORY DATA.

Describe what you see, hear, touch, taste, or smell.

Give your observations — verbal and nonverbal:

- Supply concrete who, what, where, when, and how information.
- Specify time and place.
- Give concrete examples.
- Include facts, figures, and information from print and other sources.

> "This morning, I heard Jack say he thought the project would fly."

> "I saw you frown when Joanne asked to borrow your class notes."

3. EXPRESS THOUGHTS.

Say what you think — believe, interpret, expect.

> "I believe we can meet the schedule if we give it all we've got."

> "It's my impression you're really swamped with work right now."

Document — link interpretations to sensory data (observations). This lets others know how you have drawn your conclusions.

> "There are six days left. I believe we can meet the schedule if we give it all we've got."

> "The tone of your voice gives me the impression you're really swamped with work right now."

4. SHARE FEELINGS.

Disclose your emotions directly.

- Simply share your emotions. Try to state your emotions without using the word "feel." That will help avoid confusing a feeling with a thought.

> "I'm frustrated about our progress," rather than, "I feel frustrated . . . "

> "I'm pleased with my grade," rather than, "I feel pleased. . . "

- Avoid using the common phrase, "I feel that . . . " This usually disguises a thought or want and does not clearly report an emotion.

Directly acknowledging and giving words to emotions will help you:

- Act on — rather than act out — emotions, managing tough situations.
- Ground and effectively discharge negative affect — freeing you to move on.
- Add power to your communication.

5. DISCLOSE WANTS.

Directly express your desires for Self, Other(s), and Stakeholders.

> "I want to receive credit for this project."
>
> "I would like for you to be able to reach your goal."
>
> "I'd like for the neighbors not to be irritated."

Note — distinguish wants *from* others with wants *for* other(s) — your interests and your support for others' interests.

Disclosing Wants:

- Reduces hidden agenda.

- Builds relationship — acknowledges (supports) others' interests.

- Makes issues more negotiable, less demanding.

- Does not guarantee that you will get all your wants, but puts them on the table for negotiation.

6. STATE ACTIONS

State what you have done, are doing, or will do.

> "My mind was somewhere else, and I really didn't hear what you said."
>
> "I'll check with Sarah, then get back to you before noon."
>
> "If that offends you, I won't kid you about that again."

Owning your own behavior says you are:

- Aware

- Responsible/Accountable (trustworthy)

- Committed

Be aware of the difference between saying, "I might," "I could," or "I want to," and clearly committing yourself to future action, by saying "I will." Commitment to act distinguishes Skill # 6 (committed actions) from Skill # 5 (more tentative wants, wishes and desires).

Caring behavior matches your experience with congruent words and actions.

A NOTE ABOUT THE SKILLS

The skills are numbered for convenient identification, not for use in a sequence. Apply them in any order as you share information about yourself.

COMMUNICATION STYLES AND TALKING SKILLS

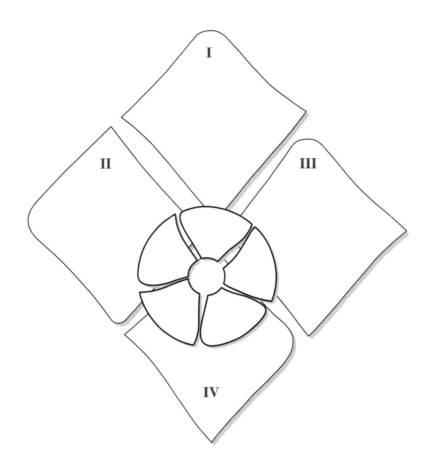

The talking skills correspond with the Communication Talking Styles.

Consider the skills separately:

- Describing Sensory Data is associated with Small Talk and Shop Talk.
- Stating Actions by themselves can revert to Control Talk.
- Expressing Thoughts hovers in Search Talk.

Consider the skills combined:

- Sharing Feelings and Disclosing Wants are essential ingredients of Straight Talk.
- All the talking skills in combination support Straight Talk.

CARING ABOUT YOURSELF

Consider These Points:

- Wherever you go, you can use your Awareness Wheel. To use it, ask yourself, "What am I experiencing right now?"

- Self-awareness is the most important resource you bring to any issue or situation.

- Self-awareness increases self-control.

- You can use your Awareness Wheel to reduce stress, manage tension, and resolve issues.

- Connecting with all parts of your experience gathers fragmented information and releases blocked energy.

- The more parts of your Wheel you disclose, the clearer your message.

- Partial awareness discounts self and others and yields poor outcomes.

- Fear and self-doubt block information and action.

- Knowing yourself is not the same as being selfish and self-centered.

Tips:

- Use the skills in any sequence.

- Know that an effective message does not need to be lengthy. Use the talking skills to send multi-part messages — three or more parts of your Awareness Wheel in 30 seconds or less. (A multi-part message is much clearer than a message that goes on and on in one zone.)

- Expand awareness before taking action.

- Increase your choices with self-awareness/information.

- Ask yourself, "Are my actions (what I say and do) consistent with all parts of my Wheel?"

- Act congruently on your self-awareness to create energy, strength, and health.

EXERCISE: SOMEONE YOU WANT TO INFLUENCE — REVISITED

Instruction

1. Turn to page xii in the Preface to the pre-assessment exercise, "Someone You Want to Influence" (about something of importance to you). Recall the person and what it was that you wanted to influence him or her about.

2. Time yourself again; take four minutes. Only this time use the Awareness Wheel (below) to stimulate and organize what you want to say to this person.

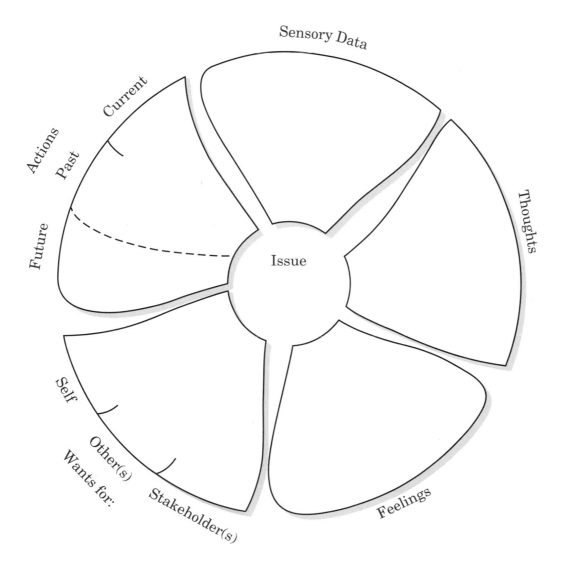

Exercise continued on next page

3. Code the Pre-Assessment: Turn again to page xii and code each of your original statements on the page with an S=Sensory Data, T=Thought, F=Feeling, W=Want, and A=Action.

4. Compare: How many and which zones of the Wheel did you cover in your pre-assessment? Between the two exercises, how does the quality of information compare?

5. Think about the person you want to influence and how he or she would be most responsive to your message.

6. Number the zones of the Wheel in the sequence you believe would work best.

7. Pick a time and place to talk to this person.

EXERCISE: USE YOUR TALKING SKILLS

Share something important about yourself with someone (for example, tell about a significant change in your life, an impactful experience, or a personal issue you are struggling with). Use the talking skills.

Prepare: Fill out the Wheel below about the topic.

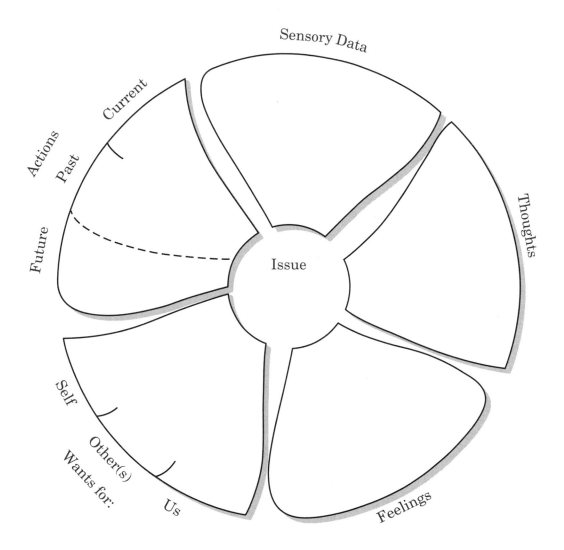

Rehearse: You may want to use the Awareness Wheel skills mat.

Prepare the person: Tell him or her you have something you want to tell about yourself. The person needs only to listen; you are not looking for any kind of response or answer.

Afterwards: Consider your use of the skills. (Use the questionnaire on the next page.)

USE OF TALKING SKILLS

Instructions

Mark each item twice: first with an X for current habit; next with an O for desired practice.

When you have a serious conversation with another person, how often do you:

	Almost never				Very often
1. Speak for self?	1 2 3 4 5 6
2. Speak for other (tell person what he/she should think, feel, want, or do)?	1 2 3 4 5 6
3. Describe sensory data (say what you observe)?	1 2 3 4 5 6
4. Express your thoughts?	1 2 3 4 5 6
5. Share your feelings?	1 2 3 4 5 6
6. Disclose your wants for self?	1 2 3 4 5 6
7. Disclose your wants for (not from) him or her?	1 2 3 4 5 6
8. State your current or past actions (own your behavior)?	1 2 3 4 5 6
9. State your future actions (make commitments)?	1 2 3 4 5 6
10. Say one thing, but think, feel, want, or do another?	1 2 3 4 5 6

Action Plan

Circle the numbers of one or two skill-items to focus on improving.

4

INTERACTIVE PRINCIPLE & GUIDES

When Demands Exceed Resources
Use Your Awareness
Breathe and Center

INTERACTIONS AND STRESS

Principle: When the demands of a situation appear to exceed your available resources to cope, your personal pressure (stress) increases.

This explains why facing new or unresolved issues often causes stress. It is also the reason that you feel anxious when you think you are losing control of a situation.

As an issue arises or a difficult exchange occurs, your response urge may be to *flee* from the situation, *freeze* in place, or *fight* to take control of it. Your language and nonverbals at that moment reflect your choice. You may hover in Small and Shop Talk (flee), get quiet (freeze), or move into Control, Fight, or Spite Talk, attempting to force change in the situation (fight).

You can experience pressure in a situation regarding an issue, whether the demands of the issue are *real* or *imagined*. In either case, your body registers the strain — your vision narrows, your breathing becomes more shallow and rapid, the muscles tighten in your upper body, neck, and face — as your communication and nonverbals become more tense. Others read your stress and take on your tension, too, increasing the pressure in the whole interaction.

That is why it is important to manage yourself when you experience pressure in your interactions about issues.

MANAGING YOURSELF

Although you may not be able to control when, where, and how issues arise, you can control how you respond to them. You can increase or decrease the pressure on yourself and others.

Guide: Use Your Awareness

A foundation for managing yourself in stressful situations is to tune into your awareness. Examples of early warning *cues of pressure* come from:

■ External sensory data — from others

   Nonverbally — higher-pitched voice, physical crowding or distancing, rolling of the eyes or a sneer

   Verbally — tense or angry words and phrases

■ Internal sensory data — from your own body

   Muscle tension (even slight pain) in your neck, shoulders, or chest; headache; stomach ache

Other zones of your Awareness Wheel can signal stress, too.

■ Thoughts — thinking that you are stuck or blocked

■ Feelings — feeling fear, distrust, or disappointment

■ Wants — experiencing thwarted desires, wishes

■ Actions — using an ineffective talking style (Spite Talk) in an exchange

Guide: Breathe and Center

As soon as you are aware of the pressure cues, use them as a signal for you to breathe and center, consciously and in the moment. This is an important step in managing yourself, as you respond to a stressful issue or interaction.

Centering may seem counter-intuitive, yet the effect is that of relaxing and rebalancing your physiology. Being centered:

■ Gives you increased physical strength, flexibility, and energy to cope.

■ Prepares you to respond to stressors more effectively, both intrapersonally and interpersonally.

■ Facilitates expanded awareness and open communication.

■ Tends to have a calming, relaxing effect on the others.

Your center is just below the middle of your abdomen, a natural midpoint of physical balance from which you can exert minimum effort for maximum results. This axletree is located about one-and-a-half to two inches below your navel and inside your body, from the front, one-third of the way back toward your backbone. The muscular and skeletal structure and effort necessary to sit, stand, move, and manage yourself in an interaction is optimally balanced above and below this midpoint.

When you are at center you are in an alert yet relaxed state. Your muscles throughout your body do not work against themselves, causing inefficiency and fatigue. Rather, from your physical power center, you can do your best at many things, such as playing a sport or relating to another person.

> To manage your own anxiety, pressure, or tension and to help calm others' anxiety and tension in any challenging circumstance, **go to center.**

How to Go to Center

To learn to go to center the easiest way:

1. Take a deep, relaxing breath through your nose, with your mouth closed.

2. Notice how as you breathe diaphragmatically, your body relaxes and seems to settle or re-balance itself naturally into your mid-section. This releases accumulated tension in your upper body and reconfigures your nonverbal presence.

3. Use your hand, as you breathe, to press gently into your stomach at the point about one-and-a-half to two inches below your navel to help you recognize and experience your center.

You can center yourself in any posture: sitting, standing, or lying down.

Breathing diaphragmatically helps you center. However, with practice, you can go to center without taking a breath, simply by letting yourself relax instantly down to your midpoint.

Points to Consider

■   Research on stress indicates that the way a person responds to and deals with pressure is much more important to well being than any particular source of the stress itself.

■   When you feel pressure in an interaction, the tendency is to rely on old comfortable yet ineffective (freeze, flee, or fight) habits, rather than to use new skills. By using your awareness and by breathing and centering, you can alter your physiological state, making your new skills more operational.

■   On average, the human brain weighs about two percent of total body weight, but consumes about twenty percent of the oxygen a person inhales. Oxygen is the brain's major nutrient. Breathing and centering in stressful situations increases oxygen to the brain when it is most needed.

- Breathing and centering can support your own comfortable silence when that is appropriate during an exchange.

- When centered, you are relaxation-in-motion, relating from your power center without trying to be powerful. Your nonverbals reflect your presence — radiating dynamic, relaxed strength, rather than static tension and stress. Managing yourself helps you manage the situation.

EXERCISE: BREATHE AND CENTER — EXPAND YOUR AWARENESS

Instructions

Choose a current, unresolved issue. Use your Awareness Wheel skills mat to process the issue with Self-talk.

As you move about the mat, let yourself breathe deeply (especially when you experience any anxiety or tightness in your upper body — face, neck, chest, stomach, arms, and hands). As you breathe, let yourself relax into your center, and feel your feet and total body become more solidly grounded as you step into your experience.

As you breathe and center occasionally, let yourself continue to move about the Wheel, augering deeper into the issue and expanding your awareness. Be honest with yourself and allow the various parts of your awareness to interconnect and inform you.

Discover how much easier it is to expand your awareness and create a congruent next step (future action) by breathing, centering and relaxing as you manage yourself.

SECTION III

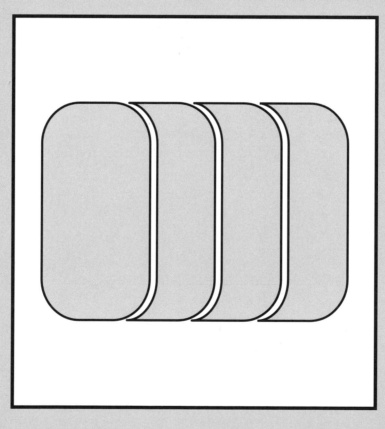

5

INTERACTIVE PRINCIPLE & GUIDES

Every Body Speaks Its Mind
Establish Rapport
Play Hot or Cold

SELF AWARENESS PLUS OTHER AWARENESS

Effective interpersonal communication takes more than self-awareness and clarity of talking. It also requires that you *attend* to other people's feedback and *adjust* your own behavior so that you can connect and exchange information. Depending on your effectiveness with all these processes, you build or dampen relationships.

Your level of awareness of others makes the difference in your ability to attend and adjust. You can think of your other-awareness as operating like a complex servo-mechanism that traverses new, uncharted, and or even difficult terrain by scanning the environment for feedback and adjusting its approach.

Principle: Every Body Speaks Its Mind — Nonverbally

As you relate to someone, in any style of communication, the other person responds to you. (And you in turn respond to him or her — no one cannot *not* communicate.) Besides verbally interacting, each person's body constantly speaks its mind through subtle and not-so-subtle nonverbals, such as small facial changes, gestures, head movements and posture shifts; other nonverbals include rate, pitch, volume, and tone of voice.

Most nonverbals are spontaneous and hard to control consciously. They often reflect emotion and operate outside the sender's awareness. However, these nonverbal behaviors from others serve as your interpersonal sensory data base — your feedback.

Body Signature

Everyone has a *body signature* — a reoccurring pattern or range of large and small nonverbal behaviors that are unique to that person. For example, some people, who are quite expressive, tend to use more space around them and large gestures to communicate. Other less expressive people are more contained or subdued in their use of space and in their gestures. Their nonverbals are more subtle.

As you get to know someone, you come to recognize the body signature — his or her individual pattern of nonverbal behaviors. You notice, for instance, the nonverbal cues in the person associated with calm, stressful, or exciting situations.

Points About Nonverbal Messages

Consider these points as you make use of nonverbal information from others in your exchanges.

- *Nonverbals precede verbals.* People will show you their response before they tell it. For example, when you ask a question, if you watch as well as listen, you will typically see the answer (head movement) before you hear it.

- *Nonverbals are more powerful than verbals.* Observers usually believe what they see more than what they hear (words), whether or not the interpretation of visual data is accurate.

- *Nonverbals are implicit; words are explicit.* The nonverbals suggest what the response is.

- *Nonverbals punctuate interaction.* They tend to signal beginnings, endings, and recycling of short interactions.

Keep in Mind:

- *Nonverbals are easy to misinterpret.* No gesture by itself has a specific meaning. Every gesture can have multiple meanings. And no one gesture means the same thing every time. Nonverbals depend in large part on context. For example, crossed "closed" arms can mean, "I'm not interested," or "I'm sitting on a chair without comfortable arm rests," or perhaps "It's cold in here and I'm hugging myself to stay warm." When you do not understand something you see nonverbally, ask for clarification.

- *Nonverbals serve as the basis for judging congruence.* A match or mismatch can occur between communication channels — between what a person says (verbally) and does (nonverbally). When a mismatch seems to be going on, check it out.

Attending to others' nonverbals (such as their smiling, frowning, head nodding, changes in breathing, or small movements of pulling back or leaning forward) provides you with much of the feedback you need for choosing, calibrating, or altering your own communication.

RAPPORT — BEING IN SYNC

The most important on-going dynamic between two people is rapport. When two individuals are in sync — in alignment, similarity, accord, commonality — you can see it first in their bodies (similar posture and nonverbal behavior) or in a common language (use of similar jargon or metaphors). They mirror or reflect each other in basic and subtle ways. Their physical movements and words seem to connect, displaying trust and liking.

On the other hand, when two people are out of sync, they lack basic rapport with each other. Again, you can see it in their bodies and behavior. They do not match. Rather, they seem to grate on each other — creating dissonance and distrust as they attempt to relate in awkward, uncertain, uncomfortable and uncoordinated ways. They seem out of step with one another and on different wave lengths.

Guide: Establish and Maintain Rapport

Generally, most of us enjoy living, working, and playing with people with whom we share a high level of rapport. However, when these things do not go well, it is necessary to regain rapport. And, when we want to influence someone or successfully meet new people, we must establish and then maintain rapport.

The first step in establishing rapport is to look for ways to signal sameness and reduce difference (regardless of age, gender, race, ethnicity, and so on). Then, to come into sync, literally match (mirror or reflect, but not mimic) another person's behavior (verbal or nonverbal), such as speech rate or posture. In these ways, align yourself by taking your cues from the other person's lead.

Ways to Match the Other Person Include:

Activity/Behavior	Space (Closeness/Distance)
Breathing	Speech Rate/Pitch/Volume
Communication Style	Topic of Discussion
Energy Level/Mood	Words/Images/Metaphors
Facial/Body Movements	Zone of the Awareness Wheel
Posture	

Once you are in alignment (which usually takes just a few seconds), often the two of you begin to blend — mirroring and matching each other naturally. In fact, when someone is connecting with you, you can see him or her unconsciously mirroring your own behavior as well. When rapport is established, your behavior unconsciously suggests things such as, "We're alike." "You can trust me." "We're on the same side." or "I like you."

When you realize you have lost rapport with someone, consciously mirror and match again to reestablish your rapport.

People can mirror and match each other verbally and nonverbally in any style of communication. You will see both style shifts and changes in physical rapport as people:

- Negotiate the style in which they are going to relate.
- Change the topic.
- Encounter sudden dissonance between them.

Points to Consider

- It takes only a moment to align yourself physically with another person, before you engage yourself fully in the conversation.
- High rapport does not necessarily mean agreement. You can disagree with someone and still be in sync. For example, two people can disagree in Style IV and still experience rapport with one another.
- Rapport is hardest to establish with people most unlike you or with people to whom you find it difficult to relate. It develops quite naturally with people most like you.
- Sometimes the people you want to influence the most are people with whom you have the least rapport.

Results of Mirroring Others

Intentionally mirroring others will:

- Prevent you from sending negative nonverbal messages.
- Take the attention off yourself in awkward or new situations.
- Help you understand and sometimes share another person's experience.
- Enable you to avoid overpowering or underpowering the other.
- Reduce interpersonal dissonance.
- Build relationship.

Suggestions

1. Look for and build on similarities, likeness, and common ground with others. If you focus primarily on differences, your body and nonverbals will communicate rejection.
2. Match someone's words and images. Everyone has his or her own vocabulary.
3. In a meeting, mirror and match the body language of the person you want to influence (to increase your similarity and reduce difference or dissonance).

HOT OR COLD

Remember when you were a child and played a game called "Hot or Cold," "Hide the Thimble," or something similar? The rules were simple: Someone left the room and you hid an object. When the individual re-entered the room, he or she was supposed to find the hidden object based on the verbal feedback you and others in the room provided.

As the seeker moved closer to the hidden object, the others called out, "Warm!" "Hot!" or (very close) "Burning up!" If the person moved away from the object, the others would say, "You're cold!" "Ice cold!" or "Freezing!"

The game was fun, and the seeker would readily find the object as long as he or she:

> 1) Was given accurate feedback

> 2) Attended to and used the feedback

If the seeker was given inaccurate information by others or did not attend to the feedback, the game became a frustrating random search without helpful information.

Interpersonal communication operates on a feedback system very much like playing the game "Hot or Cold." *Other people's nonverbals are the hot and cold feedback that give us clues as to whether what we are doing is working or not working.* The nonverbals suggest if our actions are receiving a:

> positive response — consideration, acceptance, agreement

> negative response — reluctance, rejection, disagreement

Others' nonverbals translate to "warm," "hot," "sizzling," or "cool," "cold," "freezing," respectively.

As you communicate, the other person's nonverbals reflect the effectiveness or ineffectiveness of your communication. They are as much a statement about you — the impact of your communication — as they are a statement about the other person.

Guide: Play Hot or Cold — Ask Yourself, "Is What I Am Doing Working or Not Working?"

You can generally make safe and useful *global judgment*s about whether your communication is working or not working (hot or cold) from the other person's nonverbal responses to you. Adjust accordingly. However, since nonverbals are implicit and not explicit, be careful not to read too much explicitness into them. Do not make detailed interpretations of the nonverbals.

EXERCISE: ATTENDING TO NONVERBALS

Instructions: Choose two people to observe over the next few days whom you are likely to see in both *calm* and *pressured* situations. In each circumstance, notice the subtle differences you observe in their nonverbal behavior, for example, their breathing, facial expressions (including lower lip), gestures, posture, speech rate, voice tone and volume, and use of space. Record some of your observations below.

Person #1   Person #2

EXERCISE: PLAY HOT AND COLD

Instructions: During a Small Talk or Shop Talk conversation with someone, experiment with Speaking for Other and Speaking for Self. Observe the Hot and Cold responses you receive.

1.   Shift intentionally into Control talk and Speaking for Other, by telling the person what he or she thinks, feels, or wants. As you speak for him or her, observe his or her Hot or Cold nonverbal responses to what you are saying. In all probability, you will see cold responses as you verbally crowd the other person.

2.   Begin, at some point, to Speak for Self. Watch for any changes in Hot or Cold responses to what you are saying. (Sometimes it takes a few minutes, during which you Speak for Self, for the person to respond in a way that is less guarded or protected than what he or she displayed when you used the Speak-for-Other, intrusive approach.)

Notice how easy it is to *escalate* the tension in a conversation, simply by Speaking for Other. If the other person becomes defensive, shift to Speaking for Self to *de-escalate* the tension. Record any observations below.

6

THE LISTENING CYCLE MAP

Explorative Listening Skill
Attentive Listening Skills

ISSUES AND EFFECTIVE LISTENING

In a conversation with another person about an issue, in which you both have a stake or in which the other person wants to share his or her experience (perhaps to seek your counsel), both of you contribute to the process. In such situations, ask yourself these questions about your listening behavior:

- To what extent do I inhibit, contaminate, or encourage the other's information — the person's experience of the issue?

- Is my intent to control or connect?

- Do I push for *agreement* or pursue *understanding* (on which to build agreement)?

When an issue is at hand, the goals of effective listening include:

- To *respect* (care about) the other person, by hearing, in an uncontaminated way, the person's "story."

- To *understand* the other person's experience accurately.

- To *discover* useful information.

- To *build* trust and relationship.

Different Situations Call for Different Listening Styles

The key to effective listening is to manage yourself by choosing a listening style appropriate to the situation.

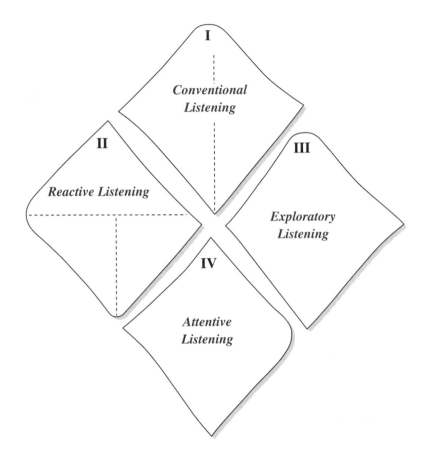

- Style I, Conventional Listening, is appropriate for non-issue situations.

- Style II, Reactive Listening, fits when you want to gain selective information, to formulate a quick reaction.

- Style III, Explorative Listening, uses questions to gather important information about issues.

- Style IV, Attentive Listening encourages others to lead you to their core information.

Your styles of communication — how you talk and listen — determine the quality of information exchanged and the state of your relationship with the person present. This chapter focuses on the listening skills associated with Styles III and IV, the two best listening styles for connecting with others in non-routine, complicated, and conflict-resolving situations.

EXPLORATIVE LISTENING — STYLE III

Semi-Open Style

Explorative Listening is a semi-open style (described on pages 23-24 in the chapter, "Communication Styles"). This style helps to gain an overview, explore facts and causes, and examine or generate possibilities. Its appropriate use occurs in searching for significant information about complex or non-routine issues.

Questions — The Nature of Explorative Listening

Explorative Listening revolves around asking different types of questions. Depending on their structure, the questions probe, guide, or stimulate answers. Sometimes a particular line of questioning goes on; other times more open, general questions seek answers. *The structure of the question limits or expands the degree of openness in the conversation and the kind of information gained.*

In the process, as the listener asks questions, knowingly or unknowingly, the listener pursues his or her own agenda more than the talker's agenda to discover information. Sometimes this is appropriate. Other times, the questioner gets in the way of finding quality information.

Explorative Listening behaviors include asking :

> *Closed Questions* — severely limiting responses to "yes" or "no,"
> "right" or "wrong," "good" or "bad," and so on.
>
> *Open Questions* — focusing, but leaving the response to the talker.

The listener may ask variations on these types of questions, such as querying about more extensive options (in not quite so closed questions) or seeking an estimate on a continuum of possibilities (in less open questions).

Use Open Questions to Focus on any Zone of the Awareness Wheel

Combine "Who," "What," "Where," "When," and "How," (but not "Why") with zones of the Awareness Wheel to form focused open questions.

The Awareness Wheel can function as a listening tool to help you organize and fill in missing information.

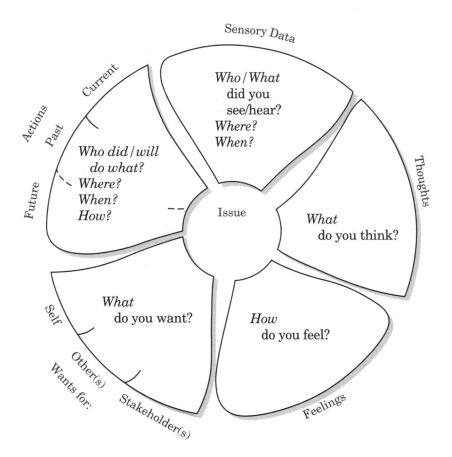

Special Uses of Explorative Listening

This listening style helps particularly in structuring a conversation with people who:

Talk *too little* — need prompting to tell their story completely.

Talk *too much* — need organization to help them focus.

Positive Impacts of Explorative Listening

Open questions focus the conversation. They often:

- Fill in missing information.
- Clarify unclear/confusing parts.
- Confirm information (for example, the accuracy of an interpretation or summary).
- Keep a conversation going.

Negative Impacts of Asking Open Questions

Open questions, intentionally or unintentionally, can interfere with gaining core information by:

- Disrupting the spontaneous flow of a talker's story.
- Directing the conversation away from critical information.
- Shifting the focus from the talker's source experience to the listener's secondary knowledge. (This can occur particularly when the listener is an "expert.")
- Influencing and possibly contaminating information.
- Anticipating the next questions, rather than attending to immediate data.

Points to Consider About Asking Open Questions

- Think about when to ask questions. Many people ask questions too early and too much in a listening situation. (Some people think listening means solving problems so their job as a listener is to guide the talker to a solution, or come up with the answer. As a result, they start asking questions prematurely.)
- Consider the necessity for questions. (Some people believe that they show their interest in a problem by taking over the conversation with questions. As a result, they often frustrate the talker.)
- Questions place considerable work and responsibility on the listener. Realize that premature or too much questioning confuses whose responsibility it is for information to be known. Later, a listener can ask (blaming), "Why didn't you tell me that earlier?" The talker can reply (also blaming), "I don't know. You never asked me."

The value of a question is determined by the quality of information it produces. Explorative listening, through questioning, helps focus information, which can be useful in certain situations that require structuring.

EXERCISE: ASK OPEN QUESTIONS

Instructions

Interview someone about an event or issue of importance to him or her. Use the Awareness Wheel (below) and ask open questions to fill out the person's story.

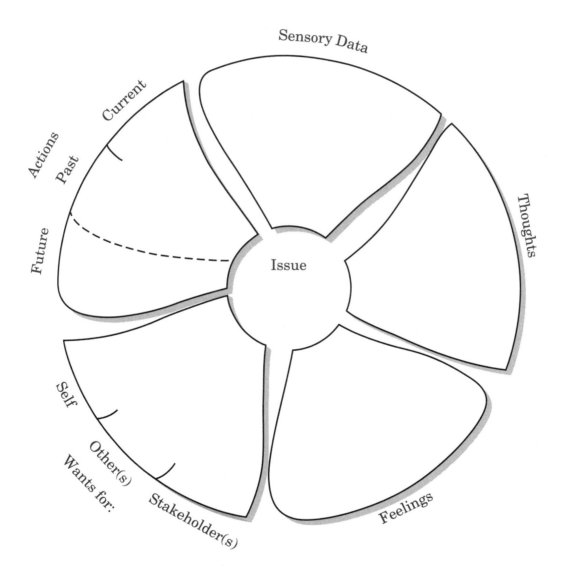

THE LISTENING CYCLE

The Listening Cycle is a map of listening skills. In addition to its description of the skills, it provides a guide for applying the skills that helps particularly when an important, complex, or stressful issue is at hand. With its use, you maximize your listening effectiveness.

The Listening Cycle begins with skills for Attentive Listening. Then it moves to the fifth skill of Asking Open Questions, presented earlier in this chapter as the mainstay of the Explorative Listening Style.

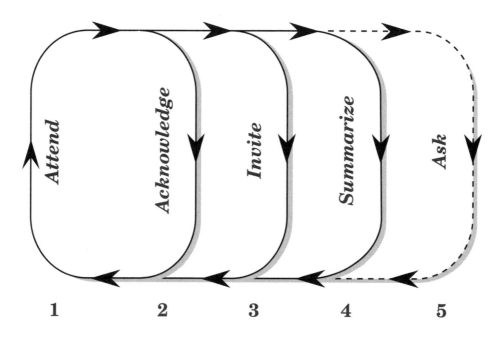

Attend   *Acknowledge*   *Invite*   *Summarize*   *Ask*

1   2   3   4   5

ATTENTIVE LISTENING — STYLE IV

Open Style

Attentive Listening is an open style. Here the listener intends to discover information, by encouraging the talker to speak freely about his or her full awareness. The behaviors of Attentive Listening enhance the flow and quality of information. The listener tries to go into the talker's world and experience the situation as he or she does.

In Attentive Listening, you use four skills to tune into the talker, to be accurate about what he or she says, and to connect with that person, rather than to direct, manipulate, or correct the talker's experience.

ATTENTIVE LISTENING SKILLS

1. ATTEND — Look, Listen, Track

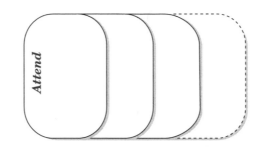

Attending means you give the talker your careful attention — you adjust your body posture to mirror the talker and listen with your eyes and ears. By fully attending, you drink in sensory data that become the basis for understanding and connecting with the talker.

How to Attend:

- *Observe* the talker's nonverbals, which display shifts in posture, facial expression, and energy.

- *Listen* to the sounds of the words — tone of voice, rate, and volume of speech.

- *Track* the zones disclosed of the Awareness Wheel. Notice the content, the choice of the words — what the talker tells you —from the various zones. (See the graphic on the next page.)

Attending Tips

- Set you own concerns aside temporarily (you won't lose them) and stop other activity that is, or could appear to be, distracting.

- Breathe (silently) and center to help you shift from your previous activity into attending and mirroring behaviors.

- Mirror the talker (sit/sit; stand/stand).

- Make eye contact as you listen.

- Let the talker set the pace. (This signals your availability, receptivity, and interest.)

- Watch for congruence/incongruence — the match between the person's words and his or her nonverbals. (For example, the person says, "I'm pleased" and looks pleased; or says, "I'm happy" but looks or sounds sad.)
- Notice if any zones on the Awareness Wheel are not stated.

To Track:

Follow the content of the talker according to the zones of the Awareness Wheel.

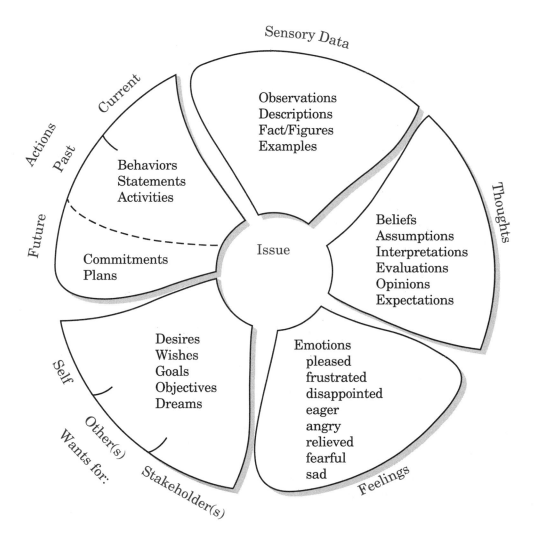

2. ACKNOWLEDGE — Other's Experience

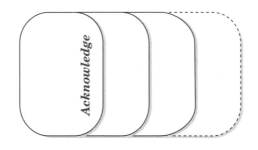

Acknowledgements are small fragments — words, phrases, or brief sentences — that attempt to note accurately what the talker is experiencing. To acknowledge means you:

■ Show respect for and acceptance of the talker's experience as being valid and legitimate for him or her. (This does not necessarily mean you agree. Your experience may be totally different.)

■ Go with — rather than go against — the talker's experience. (To do this, you try to connect with or even amplify rather than block, sidetrack, or react to the experience.) It shows the talker that he or she has your moment-to-moment attention and understanding.

■ Formulate brief "voice-overs" as the talker speaks. These do not disrupt the talker but rather act like sonar, confirming that you are on target. If you are off course, the talker will correct or calibrate your understanding.

How to Acknowledge

■ Reflect the part of the talker's Wheel, as he or she speaks, for example:

"Colorful." (Data); "Big decision." (Thought); "Frustrating." (Feeling)

"Really want that." (Want); or "Hard work" (Action)

■ Use, if possible, just one word to reflect, for example:

"Bummer." (Thought); "Scary." (Feeling)

■ Include nonverbal behaviors, such as:

gestures (for example, nodding your head),

facial expressions,

supportive sounds.

■ Pay particular attention to and verbalize unstated *feelings* and *wants*:

> Sore spots — anger, frustration (negative energy)
>
> Soft spots — fear, hurt, vulnerability
>
> Unfulfilled wants
>
> Blocked desires
>
> Hot spots — excitement (positive energy)

■ Watch the talker's response for small hot or cold nonverbals. They will signal the accuracy and impact of your acknowledgement. When you touch the right chord, the talker will be energized (warm to hot). If you are off track, you will see his or her nonverbals freeze, or signal cool.

Points About the Skill of Acknowledging

■ Attending and acknowledging builds bridges. It shows you care about that person and affirms his or her right to talk and be understood. These are powerful forces for building rapport and for collaborating.

■ Acknowledging helps you stand in the talker's shoes.

■ It is important in the moment, when you acknowledge, to go where the talker's energy is — data, thoughts, emotions, wants, actions — not where your energy is as a listener.

■ Acknowledgements reduce the talker's resistance by your offering no resistance.

■ Acknowledging what the other person is experiencing is often all that is necessary to connect and create understanding.

3. INVITE — More Information

Inviting means that *you say or do something that encourages the talker to continue spontaneously talking about whatever it is he or she wants to tell you.* The effect of an invitation is that the talker, not the listener, chooses where to go next.

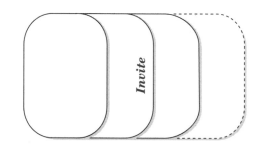

How to Invite:

- Realize that inviting can take three forms:

    Gentle *command:*

    "Continue."

    "Say more."

    Wide open *question* (not a focused open question):

    "What else?"

    "Anything more?"

    Statement:

    "I'd like to hear more."

    "This is hard for me to hear, but I'd like you to continue."

Invite When:

- There is a pause.
- You experience the urge to react, disagree, or advise.
- You want to ask a question (closed or focused open question).

Keep inviting — Two, Three, or More Times:

- You will receive richer, more complete information.
- Continue inviting until the talker says he or she has nothing more to add. At that point you know the story is complete, and that it is the time for you to begin to ask questions or talk yourself.

- Sometimes the talker will say he or she has nothing more to add, or will pause and go on to say, "But," and then give you a piece of informational gold.

Points About the Skill of Inviting

- Inviting operationalizes the 80/20 rule. The listener encourages and allows the talker to connect with his or her own uncontaminated experience regarding an issue or situation.

- Inviting is a particularly useful skill when a talker wants to tell his or her story, but for various reasons you are prone to direct or take over for the talker.

- Giving a person maximum choice and freedom to tell his or her story usually produces the richest information, most efficiently.

- Inviting, like peeling an onion a layer at a time, will take you deeper into the core of a person's experience.

- Essentially, each time you invite, you let the talker know, "What you are saying is important to me. I have time to listen. I want you to keep talking." As a result, the talker relaxes, trust grows, and he or she is more likely to tell you what is really going on — what he or she really thinks, feels, or wants.

- Typically, after receiving several invitations, the talker reveals information not yet said but important to the issue.

- Rather than playing a guessing game with questions, inviting lets the talker lead you to the critical information. Until the talker has no more to add, questions are premature and mainly distract and sidetrack.

4. SUMMARIZE — to Ensure Accuracy

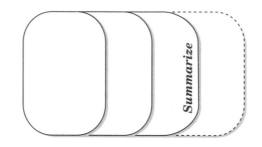

Summarizing demonstrates to the talker that you have accurately understood what he or she has said. It ensures that the message sent has been received accurately, whether or not you agree with what the other has said.

How to Summarize:

- Repeat in your own words what you have just heard to be the other person's points.

    "Let me see if I've got what you just said."

    "I'd like to run back what you've just told me to be sure I've got it."

- Be complete, yet *do not add to* (make inferences about) *or subtract from* (leave parts out of) the original message.

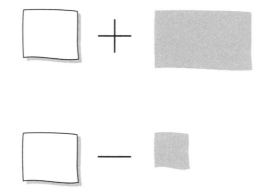

- Watch the talker's nonverbal response to your summary, such as head nodding or a frown, for hot or cold signals of your accuracy.

- Ask for confirmation or clarification of your summary if the talker's response is unclear or uncertain.

■ Re-cycle a summary more than once until both of you are satisfied that the message sent equals the message received.

Summarize When You:

Have an important issue at hand and believe understanding is critical

Think misunderstanding seems to be occurring

Experience stressful exchanges

Want to prioritize issues

Want to clarify perspectives

Want to resolve conflicts

Confirm an action plan

Points About the Skill of Summarizing

■ People like to be heard accurately. Summarizing builds confidence, trust, and relationship.

■ Interrupting someone to summarize his or her points is rarely seen as rude. Usually, quite the opposite, it is considered respectful.

■ Summarizing punctuates a complicated conversation, assuring understanding before proceeding.

■ A talker can ask the listener for a summary as well, without waiting for the listener to initiate one. ("Can you tell me what you've heard me say?")

Tip

Avoid saying, "I understand what you mean." (The statement is often used to take charge of or control a conversation, without real understanding.) Rather, demonstrate your understanding with an accurate summary.

5. ASK — Open Questions

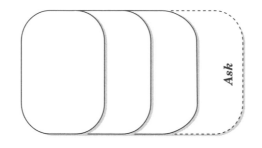

After you have helped a person tell you his or her concern or story as completely as possible using the Attentive Listening Skills 1 to 4 (described above), you may want to fill in missing information or clarify confusing parts. To do this, ask the open explorative question of "Who," "What," "Where," "When," and "How," but not "Why." (Why usually implies blame and raises defenses.) Consider asking questions from all the zones of the Awareness Wheel.

> "Who was there?"
>
> "When did this occur?"
>
> "What did you think was going on?"
>
> "How did you feel?"
>
> "What do you want for Jim (based on his interests)?"
>
> "What are you going to do about it?"

In general, ask questions least and last. They are helpful when you want to structure and limit information. Usually though, if given the chance, most people tell their story best with acknowledgements and invites rather than with probing questions.

(See pages 83-86 in this chapter for more information on asking open questions.)

APPLY THE LISTENING CYCLE

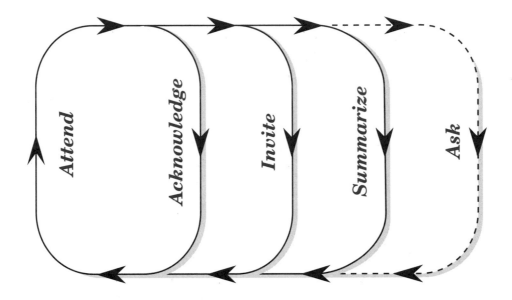

The Listening Cycle combines and guides the skills for most effective listening. While each of the five skills can be used independently and in any order as you listen, you heighten your ability to understand another by following a pattern for applying the skills. This is especially significant when you are discussing a complex or stressful issue.

■ Notice in the Listening Cycle, the heavy lines that circulate among the Attentive Listening skills —Attend, Acknowledge, Invite, and Summarize. Recycling these skills, in any order, produces the highest quality of useable information possible.

■ Remember that the Listening Cycle shows Ask (Open Questions) positioned last (and set off by dotted lines). This is to remind you to use questions least and last.

■ Note that two skill combinations are particularly useful:

Acknowledge and Invite

Summarize and Invite

HOW TO USE THE LISTENING CYCLE SKILLS MAT

Skills mats are tools to help you learn communication skills faster and better. They combine left and right-brain activity so you can practice and be coached on the skills.

The Listening Cycle mat helps you focus on and choose listening behaviors. It also guides you to recycle the skills that are connected by the solid lines.

How to Use the Floor Mat:

- Set the mat so that the words "Listening Cycle" (at the bottom) face you as you look down. The skill words are perpendicular to you.

- Step on the mat, but be sure it does not slip on the floor when you step on it.

- Start by standing with your right foot on "Attending" as you attend — listen to and observe the talker.

- When you use another skill, move your right foot to the name of the skill. (Use just one foot to step clearly on the skill; keep the other foot behind you for balance. This helps show which skill you intend to be practicing as you move among them.)

- Experiment with different skills and combinations of skills.

- Fold "Ask" Open Questions under the mat to practice listening without using questions.

- Call **Time Out** at any point, and step off the mat. (Perhaps what you are hearing floods you, or you need a break.) Be sure to Check Process (see below) with the other person and reschedule a time and place to continue your listening, so that you do not discount him or her.

- Step to **Check Process** on the mat at any point and say, "I want to check the process." Then continue by saying for example, "What skills am I over-emphasizing or missing? Is it someone else's turn to do the listening?"

Suggestions for Coaching Someone on the Listening Floor Mat:

- Ask if the listener wants coaching during the exercise. If so, coach. If not, do not coach.

- Give audible suggestions, as well as foot taps, to the person doing the listening. For example, say, "Acknowledge," if you think the listener should do so. (The listener is often looking at the talker and does not see foot taps.)

- Watch the talker to see hot or cold responses when the listener summarizes. Use your observation for feedback to the listener.

CARING ABOUT OTHERS AND STAKEHOLDERS

When you use the Listening Cycle, you set your own concerns aside temporarily as you allow and encourage the other person to express his or her concerns fully. In the process, you demonstrate care for that person. Counting the other:

■ Gets to the center of issues faster with less interpersonal stress.

■ Supports (energizes) the talker to disclosure and share critical information.

■ Pursues understanding before taking action.

■ Earns you the right to be heard after you have listened to the other person tell his or her full story.

■ Allows you to relate more constructively to the other's legitimate concerns.

■ Creates a collaborative atmosphere for building best fit agreements based on understanding.

■ Leaves the other person feeling good about you, which develops trust and builds relationships.

EXERCISE: USING THE LISTENING CYCLE

Instructions: In a situation where you and another person are having a conversation, intentionally focus on listening using the skills that are connected by the solid lines on the Cycle — the Attentive Listening Skills.

Afterwards evaluate:

■ The general atmosphere between you

■ The quality of the information you gained

Consider your use of the skills. Use the questionnaire on the next page.

USE OF LISTENING SKILLS

Instructions

Mark each item twice: first with an X for current habit: next with an O for desired practice.

When you have a serious conversation with another person, how often do you:

	Almost never				Very often	
1. Fake listening when pre-occupied?	1	2	3	4	5	6
2. Listen briefly, then take over the discussion, giving information or solutions?	1	2	3	4	5	6
3. React defensively?	1	2	3	4	5	6
4. Not take time to listen to the other's full information?	1	2	3	4	5	6
5. Direct the conversation with questions?	1	2	3	4	5	6
6. Breathe and center to shift into attending better?	1	2	3	4	5	6
7. Attend to other's nonverbals?	1	2	3	4	5	6
8. Acknowledge what the other experiences?	1	2	3	4	5	6
9. Invite the other to continue talking?	1	2	3	4	5	6
10. Summarize the other's message to ensure accuracy and demonstrate understanding?	1	2	3	4	5	6
11. Ask Open Questions focused on zones in the Awareness Wheel?	1	2	3	4	5	6
12. Make use of others' hot and cold responses to adjust your communication?	1	2	3	4	5	6

Action Plan

Circle one or two skills (items) to focus on improving.

7

GENERAL PROCESSES

Use Full Repertoire
Lead or Follow

USE YOUR FULL REPERTOIRE OF CORE SKILLS

In life, literally (with the mats) or figuratively, you stand with 11 core communication skills in front of you in any interactive situation. You can apply the skills in any combination and sequence, anywhere, or anytime to communicate about or facilitate an important issue. The skills take you naturally into Styles III and IV.

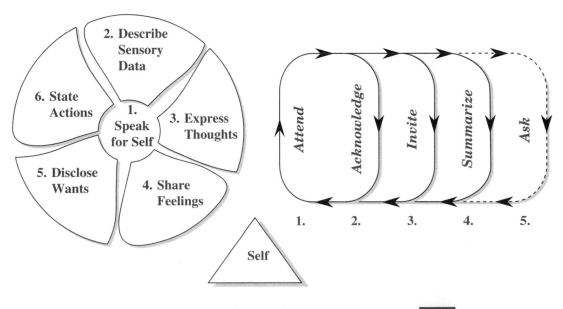

Your use of the skills does not depend on other people knowing or using the skills. Rather, you can apply your awareness and the skills, in a caring way, to influence others and your interactions positively. Think of the 11 skills as basic communication bricks from which you can build effective processes for connecting better with people in all kinds of settings. How you combine the skills produces the processes you use.

Leading and Following — General Processes

Every interaction between two or more people contains leading and following behaviors. Leading means talking or asking questions. Following means listening. When you are in an exchange with another person, whether that person is skilled in communication or not, you always have a choice, to lead or to follow. The skills can help you do both more effectively.

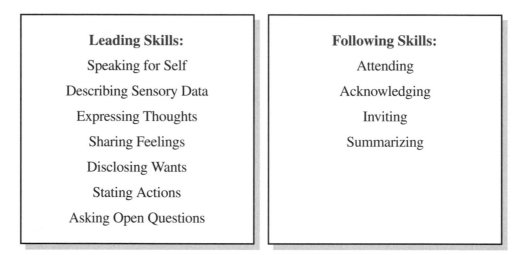

Leading Skills:

Speaking for Self

Describing Sensory Data

Expressing Thoughts

Sharing Feelings

Disclosing Wants

Stating Actions

Asking Open Questions

Following Skills:

Attending

Acknowledging

Inviting

Summarizing

Most people would rather lead (talk or ask questions) than follow (listen). At the same time, most people also want to be listened to and understood accurately. When you lead, you attempt to direct where the conversation (and talker) goes, rather than follow (listen to) where the talker goes.

Leading often results in the attempt to control the interaction, and thus the other(s). Following behaviors pursue understanding on the way to building agreement and taking action.

Advantages of Leading

Leading provides several advantages. When you lead, you:

- Direct the conversation
- Discharge affect
- Explain explicitly
- Help to reach closure
- Provide understanding of your experience
- Assert the authority of your own experience

The Fear of Leading

Sometimes people do not want to lead. They fear:

- Initiating change
- Making a commitment
- Taking responsibility, being accountable
- Offending someone
- Saying something that is seen as foolish and being criticized
- Disclosing something private

Advantages of Following

Following offers advantages, too. When you follow, you:

- Can go to the heart of the issue faster without contamination
- Reduce concern about how to respond
- Maintain and display self-control
- Earn the right to be heard
- Find that the other person usually ends up feeling better about you, as well as about himself or herself
- Create understanding and expand information

The Fear of Following

For many people, following seems counter-intuitive. They believe listening and encouraging the other person to tell his or her story will result in:

- Losing control over the other or the situation
- Showing weakness
- Being mistaken as agreeing
- Hearing about something they do not want to recognize or handle
- Being boxed in

Choosing to Lead or Follow.

Your choice about whether to lead or follow in a situation depends on several influences upon you. They include your:

- Intention(s) — what you *want* to accomplish in the situation, including whether to connect or to control

- Evaluation — whether or not you *think* *what you are doing is working or not working* — accomplishing your intentions

- Emotions — how well you are managing your own feelings, particularly *anxiety* during a challenging exchange

These influences are at work simultaneously. As you interact with someone— talk or question (lead) or listen (follow) — you also see and hear his or her *hot and cold* responses. Based on your evaluation of the sensory data, in relation to your intentions and your feelings at the moment, you decide if you should continue the process you are using.

Points to Consider

- Old-Style (increasingly ineffective) leadership revolves around unilateral leading — command and control. New-Style leadership revolves around leading and following — interactive engagement.

- In general, the most satisfying and productive interactions and relationships involve mutual (bilateral) leading and following behaviors on the part of all participants. In these situations, control is typically not an issue.

- When one person does all or most of the leading (to the dissatisfaction of the other or others), control becomes an issue. Information and relationship quality suffers.

- A savvy communicator learns when to lead and when to follow.

Tip:

- Connect (gain rapport) before attempting to lead.

EXERCISE: LEADING AND FOLLOWING

This exercise provides you with an opportunity to experiment in an interactional situation, using the full repertoire of core skills, principles, and guides presented so far.

Instructions

1. Think of a conversation about an issue or situation with another person (for example, a friend, colleague, customer, sibling, parent, child, roommate, etcetera) which you would be willing to simulate as a rehearsal or re-run. (You may also consider rehearsing the "Someone you Want to Influence" conversation, from the exercise on page 67.)

2. Position the skill mats for your (self) use with other, in the exact configuration illustrated in the graphic below.

3. Select someone (in lab or workshop) from a small group to play the role of the surrogate other (to be the person with whom you will converse. Also choose observer-coaches.

3. Brief the surrogate and observer-coaches with enough background information about the real situation so the surrogate can accurately play the other person/situation accurately. (During the course of the exercise, coach the surrogate on how to play his or her role, if he or she needs help representing the other.) (Turn the page for further instructions.)

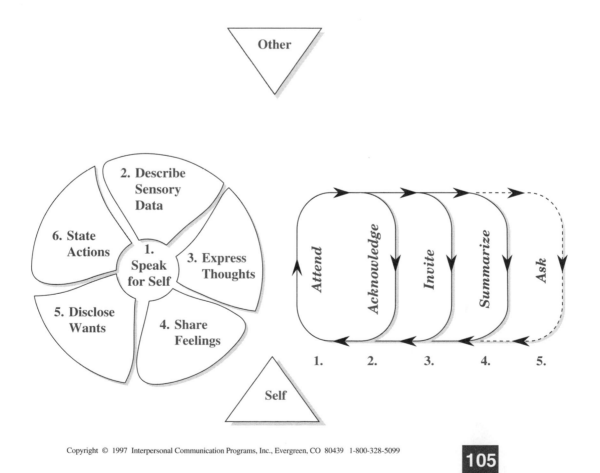

4. Tell your observer-coaches if you want feedback or not, and advise them on how you would like to be coached.

5. As you interact, see if you can stay on the mats — centered and aware, present and engaging — without slipping "off the mat" into defending or attacking, Fight Talk or Spite Talk.

6. See what you can learn about process and yourself as you experiment in the simulation.

Instructions for Other (Surrogate)

1. Make sure you have enough information (from the participant) to be able to play the other with relative accuracy and comfort.

2. As you play the role of the surrogate, respond to the participant's behavior as you experience him or her in the interaction. If what he or she is doing is not working, signal Cold. On the other hand, if what he or she is doing is working with you, signal Warm. (In a simulation like this, it is possible to lock into a role and not respond positively, regardless of how effective the participant's communication is.)

3. Do not hesitate to let yourself be influenced by the participant's actual behavior. He or she is experimenting with new behaviors.

Instructions for Observer-Coaches

1. Follow the participant's wishes if you are asked to give feedback and coach. (This is usually most helpful.)

2. Confine your coaching and feedback to process — the core skills, principles, and guides. Do not get sidetracked into discussing the *content* or proposing solutions *(outcomes).*

3. Attend to the Hot and Cold effectiveness of your feedback to the participant you are observing-coaching. Be careful not to over-coach (direct) or flood the participant with too much information. Also be sure to point out things the participant does well.

8

INTERACTIVE PRINCIPLE & GUIDE

Recognize, Stop and Shift
Resistance is your Guide

CHOICE POINT

If what you are doing in an interaction is working — you are connecting and getting a wanted response — you probably feel pleased or happy. If, on the other hand, you evaluate (in a split second) that what you are doing is not working, you are at a critical moment. You are at a choice point — a potential turning point in the interaction.

Guide: Recognize (what you are doing is not working), Stop and Shift.

What do you usually do, if what you are doing in an exchange (especially about an issue) is not working? Most people continue doing the same thing but do so harder, faster, or louder. They often unwittingly perpetuate the same unsatisfactory response.

Instead, *recognize* what is going on, and *stop and shift* to another behavior. For example, if you are leading (talking or questioning), stop and shift to following (listening). If you are following, stop and shift to leading.

Other Stop/Shifts (Besides Leading or Following Changes) Include:

- Altering Communication Style
- Changing zones of the Awareness Wheel (for example, go from focusing on thoughts to feelings or wants)
- Breathing and Centering

- Changing posture (for example, move from sitting to standing or from standing to sitting)
- Opening or closing space — move closer or farther away — the opposite of what you have been doing
- Lowering or slowing down your voice
- Changing to some other acceptable behavior

Experiment in an interaction. Change your own behavior to connect and bring a more desired change in the other person. Do not keep doing what is not working. You can apply this recognize-stop-and-shift guideline to micro-second interactions as well as to life patterns that are not working.

Interactive Corollaries

- As long as you keep doing what you are doing, you will keep getting what you are getting.
- If you want something different, you must do something different.
- It takes one person to change an interaction, and you can decide if that one person is you.
- If you change, a high probability exists that the other person will respond differently (hopefully favorably) to your change.

Self-awareness helps you recognize how you are acting and responding. By managing yourself — controlling your own contributions and responses — you are also better able to connect with others and deal with the situation.

Interconnections

You may ask yourself, "How can I remember all these things?" You do not need to remember them all; they interconnect. For example, when you change your communication style, from Fight Talk to Straight Talk, you also change your breathing. Likewise, when you breathe and center, you reduce your tension. Typically this shifts you into a more open communication style.

The key is to recognize when something is not working, and to stop and shift. Changing one part of your behavior will align other aspects as well.

Principle: Resistance is Your Guide

When you propose something (a form of change) to another person, that person may feel cautious or uncertain about it, perhaps thinking he or she is losing control of the situation. The natural tendency of the person is to become protective, disagreeable, and even defensive. His or her body begins to register its reservation (with cold responses). This is resistance. Its expression includes hesitation, objection, opposition, indifference, or rejection (all cold responses).

A typical counter response to resistance is to talk more (lead) and increase the pressure. Doing these things creates even more resistance.

As disturbing as resistance can be when you encounter it, the resistance serves an important function — it slows things down until you and the other person can understand what the change will mean and how it will impact you both. Resistance tells you where you are with that person at that moment. It often signals that you are not taking his or her wants and interests into account.

> The less you pressure someone to change, the more likely change will occur.

How to Meet Resistance

When you are leading and get two cold responses in a row, recognize that you are encountering resistance. At that point:

- **Stop, and shift.** Offer no more pressure that nourishes more resistance. Breathe and center. Shift to following, using the Attentive Listening skills, and let the person lead you to his or her reluctance.

- **Continue to follow** — acknowledge, invite, and summarize — until the point of resistance is understood fully and the person gives you critical information that must be incorporated into what you have proposed.

- **Watch for any nonverbal cue** (facial expression, alteration in posture or tone — a warm response) in the other person to see if what you are now doing is working.

- **Begin to lead again and rework** what you propose, to incorporate his or her interest.

This is how you turn resistance into a resource — an impasse into useful information.

Remember:

Do not run from resistance. Engage it; explore it; follow it. Like a reliable road sign, resistance tells you where you must go next. It will lead to what must be resolved in order to move ahead freely. This is how resistance is your guide.

Listening and Agreement

As you follow the other person into his or her world, pursuing understanding, you know that you are not necessarily in agreement. However, the other person may not realize this. That person might think you agree as he or she talks (leads).

If you think the other person is interpreting your following (listening) as meaning agreement:

> You can interject, "Please don't take my listening to mean that I am in agreement. I am just trying to understand fully what you are saying. I'm not necessarily agreeing with it."

> Or you might say, "This is hard for me to hear, but keep going."

Recognizing and freely exploring resistance is the quickest way to remove roadblocks to discover a satisfactory outcome.

Suggestions:

- Invite resistance to test the fit of something. Ask, for example, "Where are you with this?" or "In what way doesn't this fit for you?" You will move quickly to discover what is blocking things and what needs to be resolved.

- Choice reduces resistance. Allow other choices.

Consider:

- If you ignore the resistance, it will continue and interfere with a best-fit solution.

- If you do not deal with the resistance, you will waste time, and possibly end up with a false agreement or impasse.

- In communication, the shortest distance between two interactive points often means pursuing the course of *most* resistance.

- Resistance is a potential connecting point.

- Mutual, sustained resistance often escalates to Fight Talk.

EXERCISE: WHAT I DO THAT DOES NOT WORK

1. Think about what you typically do in a conversation, when you encounter resistance, that does not work.

2. Imagine, yourself in such a conversation, but instead of doing what you typically would do, use the floor skill mats to rehearse shifting into doing something more productive — engaging the resistance.

3. Look for your next opportunity to apply your new behavior.

9

CONFLICT PATTERNS MAP

Process and Outcome
Style and Process

DEALING WITH CONFLICT

Throughout your life, many of your decisions and the problems you solve affect mainly you. Perhaps in your process of reaching an outcome for them, you go through *internal conflict*.

Also, potential for *conflict* exists in any situation or event *that involves you and someone else* in your SOS system. This is so because each person's experience — sensory data, thoughts, feelings, wants, and actions — is different and unique.

The process you use in dealing with your internal (*intra*personal) conflict influences the outcome and your satisfaction with it. Likewise, when a conflict occurs between you and another person (*inter*personal conflict), how you talk and listen to that person (regardless of his or her skill in communication) makes a difference in the outcome. It also affects your satisfaction about it.

Process Yields Quality of Outcome

Once a conflict arises, regardless of *content,* it moves by *process* toward an *outcome.*

■ Any process can produce any outcome. However, certain processes yield better outcomes more frequently.

■ Various process/outcome patterns result in differing levels of satisfaction or (if a task is involved) productivity.

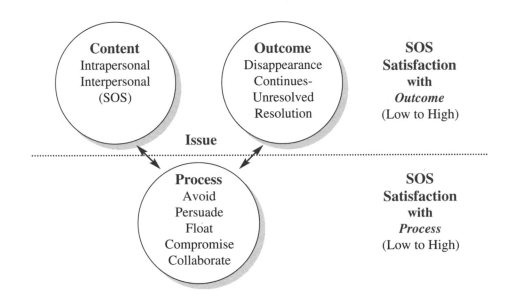

Conflict Patterns

You may find that whatever the issue or whoever it involves, you have a recurring way of dealing with it, and you often get a certain type of result. The process and outcome themselves become a conflict pattern. Perhaps you have a particular pattern for handling issues concerning you alone and a different pattern for dealing with conflicts involving someone else.

You may also realize that your satisfaction can range from low to high about the outcome you reach for your conflicts, as well as about the process you use in dealing with them. Actually, your satisfaction about each of these two aspects can differ. It could be, for example, that you are *satisfied* with the outcome of a conflict for everyone in the SOS System, but *dissatisfied* with the way it all came about — your process.

OUTCOME — A PART OF THE PATTERN

Three type of outcomes are possible for a conflict:

DISAPPEARANCE

The issue triggering the conflict goes away by itself as time passes.

CONTINUES UNRESOLVED — IN ABEYANCE

The issue continues and you alone or you and the other person stay in conflict about it. You take no action. This may range from:

- Living with indecision temporarily or indefinitely (either intrapersonally or interpersonally).
- Reaching a polarized standoff, a real impasse (interpersonally).

RESOLUTION

You take action that brings the issue to closure.

- You reach a solution (either intrapersonally or interpersonally).
- You and the other person agree to disagree (but no solution is reached).

PROCESS — A PART OF THE PATTERN

The process(es) of how you deal with conflicts internally or externally falls into five categories: avoid; persuade (coerce or capitulate); float; compromise; or collaborate.

PROCESSES ⟶	OUTCOMES
Avoid	
	Disappearance
Persuade *Coerce or Capitulate*	
	Continues Unresolved
Float	
Compromise	
	Resolution
Collaborate	

AVOID

With this process, when an issue bringing conflict occurs, you:

- Ignore it, deny its significance, or refuse to deal with it.
- Claim to be too busy.

If the conflict involves another person, in addition to the above, you may

- Skirt around it, change the subject, or refuse to discuss it
- Smooth it over with chit chat, or joke about it (Small Talk)

Impact of Avoiding:

- The outcome happens by chance or default.
- Critical decisions, problems, and conflicts go unaddressed.
- You and others in the SOS system who have something at stake in the situation are usually dissatisfied.
- Issues may disappear frequently enough for you to think that avoidance is a useful strategy.

PERSUADE

With this process, in a conflicted situation, you:

- Talk yourself into a course of action, regardless of other parts of your Wheel.

When the conflict is with another, you

- Sell the other on your own thoughts, feelings or wants (Control talk).
- Attempt to direct the other's thinking (or actions?) about the issue (Reactive Listening).
- Buy in from being persuaded that the particular solution is best.
- Comply, without counting yourself, to keep the peace.

If either you or the other person do not readily give in, the conflict can escalate into an argument or fight. With this situation, you may:

- Coerce the other. You suppress the other's point of view, struggle for power and control, or push to get the other to comply (Fight Talk). The decision tends to be unilateral.
- Capitulate, yet feel angry and resentful. Possibly you may make snide remarks or do underhanded behaviors (Spite Talk). These actually continue the conflict under the surface, though it appears to be resolved.

Impact of Persuading:

- Pre-closure may occur, and though action is taken, your satisfaction often drops. (In an interpersonal conflict, the satisfaction of someone in the SOS system is low.)
- With another person, pressure can bring an "efficient-expedient" resolution, by forcing a "false agreement." Or you can both lock up and become rigid — polarizing into an impasse.
- In a relationship, the energy lessens. One person seems to win, but in the long run, both of you lose. Damage happens and negative feelings may persist; for example, resentment and distrust thrive.

FLOAT

When you use this process during a conflict, you:

- Search for solutions and do limited brainstorming.
- Skim the surface of an issue yet leave out critical parts (for example, feelings or wants).
- Never commit to take action.

If the conflict is between you and another person, you also do the float processes just described. In addition, you:

- Speculate about causes and pose possibilities (Search Talk).
- Ask safe questions or open questions (Explorative Listening).
- Give incongruent or mixed messages.

Impact of Floating:

- No closure or resolution happens — only endless talk or ruminating continues.
- Even when issues appear to be treated seriously, there is no follow-through, so nothing changes unless by default.
- With this process, you operate according to 20/80 Rule rather than the 80/20 Rule (see the Introduction).
- While dealing with issues in this way may seem to be safe, the inaction is dissatisfying and, for a relationship, often harmful. (The indecision and lack of commitment breed discouragement,)

COMPROMISE

With this process, you reach a solution through trade-offs. By yourself, you

- Give up one thing to gain another.
- Often operate on partial awareness, not complete information.

When your conflict is with another person, you carry out the above, and you:

- Figure out with the other person and then willingly exchange concessions of differing importance to one another.

Impact of Compromising:

- Each person gains and loses something.
- Resolutions are conditional and often fragile. That is, if you do not keep the bargain with yourself, or if one of the two of you does not keep the bargain, the other receives license to break the agreement as well.
- You (and another person involved) tend to remember what you gave up (lost) more than what you gained (won).
- Compromise may or may not be fully satisfactory to everyone (in the SOS System).

People with the most good will — a caring attitude — and skill for processing issues have the most options. Without additional knowledge and skills, compromise is the highest level of resolution most people can achieve.

COLLABORATE

Collaboration goes beyond compromise. Internally, it means taking into account your full awareness and acting upon it. When your conflict involves others, you seek to:

- Disclose your awareness and listen to understand the other, including getting the real differences between you in the open (Straight Talk and Attentive Listening, as well as Explorative Listening).
- Create best-fit solutions to benefit everyone in the SOS system.
- Commit yourself to follow through with congruent action.

Impact of Collaborating:

- Solutions often take more time initially to achieve because they are built on understanding and consensus.
- In the long run, you save time and energy because you prevent the accumulative fall-out of poor or partial initial decisions.
- In a relationship, trust grows.
- Both the process and outcome usually yield highest possible levels of satisfaction for everyone in the SOS system.

STYLE DETERMINES PROCESS

When an issue (especially with conflict) must be resolved, a close relationship exists between communication style and process. The *communication style* being used supports the type of *process* going on, which in turn results in an *outcome* that brings more or less *satisfaction (*or *productivity)* for the various parts of the SOS system.

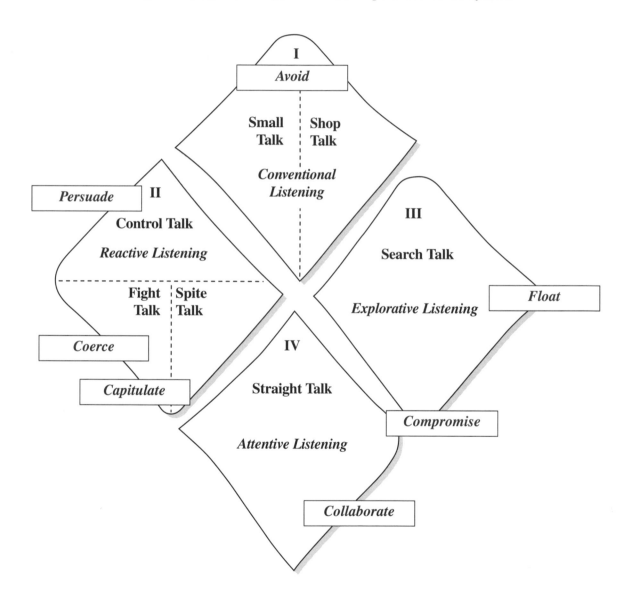

Points to Consider

■ Understanding the styles and knowing the skills give you choices in how you process conflict.

■ If the style you are using to resolve a conflict is not is not working, you can recognize its impact and shift to another style.

■ Consciously shifting your communication style will change the process going on for dealing with issues and conflict.

EXERCISE: MY PATTERNS OF CONFLICT RESOLUTION

Below is a list of processes and outcomes that make up patterns of conflict resolution.

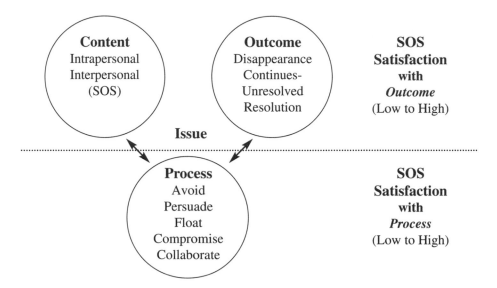

Instructions

Think about how you resolve conflicts. What are your patterns for resolving conflicts:

1. Internally?
2. With someone in your family?
3. With someone else?

Write your patterns (if helpful, note a particular example of an issue in conflict), and then rate your satisfaction level.

Example

Issue	Process	Outcome	SOS Satisfaction (Low, Medium, High)	
			Process	*Outcome*

1.

2.

3.

10

COLLABORATIVE PROCESS

Mapping an Issue

USES FOR A STRUCTURED PROCESS

In certain situations, it is helpful to follow a structured process, or model, as you work out an issue involving other people. These instances occur when you:

- Think the issue is *important, complicated,* or *controversial*
- Experience considerable *tension, conflict,* and *difference of opinion*
- Want *maximum input* from others about the issue
- Are *stuck* or *drifting*
- Seek the *best solution* in the situation

The Mapping-an-Issue process can serve as a road map for finding your way through an issue when you function in any of these capacities:

- *Participant* with another individual who does not know the skills, and you use the process (as a guide) to facilitate the two of you working out the issue or conflict.
- *Coach/Counselor/Consultant* to help another individual (again, who does not know the skills) to find the best way through his or her difficulty.
- *Facilitator/Mediator* to a two-person or a group conflict-resolution situation.

You can use the process to:

- Make decisions
- Solve problems
- Resolve conflicts

What Mapping an Issue Does

The process model presented here, called Mapping an Issue, integrates all the talking and listening skills, in Styles III and IV. Mapping an Issue is a collaborative process that counts all parts of SOS (Self, Other, Stakeholders). It works for any content, gives best-fit outcomes, and provides the highest possible satisfaction for those involved.

Content	Process	Outcome	Satisfaction
Any	Collaborative All Skills Styles III & IV	Best-Fit	Highest Possible

An Eight-Step Process

This process, which takes time and is thorough, provides a structured sequence of applying the talking and listening skills. Its eight steps are:

Step 1. Identify and Define the Issue

Step 2. Contract to Work Through the Issue

Step 3. Understand the Issue Completely

Step 4. Identify Wants

Step 5. Generate and Consider Options

Step 6. Choose Actions

Step 7. Test the Action Plan

Step 8. Evaluate the Outcome

STEP 1. IDENTIFY AND DEFINE THE ISSUE

Your task at this point is to clarify *what* the issue is, and decide *whose* issue it is.

Keep in Mind:

- An issue can arise in the awareness — sensing, thinking, feeling, wanting, or actions — of anyone involved in the SOS system.
- Style II communication often signals new or unresolved issues, in self or others.

Determine:

- *What* is the issue? You may find it helpful to decide the content type:

    Topical-Task-Technical matter

    Personal — individual matter

    Relational — interaction between people

    Group — a unit concern
- *Whose* issue is this?

    Self, Other(s), and/or Stakeholder(s)

Tips

- Use your Attentive Listening skills and ask open questions (Explorative Listening) to discover the core issue and confirm agreement.
- Often the proposed concern is not the core issue.
- State the issue. Make sure everyone involved understands and agrees that the identified issue is the real or appropriate issue.

When you are clear about the issue, proceed to Step 2.

STEP 2. CONTRACT TO WORK THROUGH THE ISSUE — ESTABLISH INTEREST, COMMITMENT, AND GROUND RULES

Have you been in a situation with someone when you wanted to talk about an issue, but a productive discussion did not occur? Perhaps it was the wrong time or place, or the other person had no real interest or commitment to resolve the matter. *Contracting is an informal agreement that sets the stage for a productive discussion by assessing everyone's interest and commitment to work on the issue and to establish operational ground rules for proceeding.*

Keep in mind:

- Without a good contract — an operational agreement and commitment to work through an issue — any discussion may be hurried, superficial, flat, or guarded, if it occurs at all.

- The more fast-paced the circumstances are or complex the issue is, the more intentional you must be about contracting, even though the other person(s) do not realize this or think it worth the time or effort.

- When a discussion is not working, ask yourself, "Do we have a *contract* to discuss this?"

To Establish a Contract:

1.   Check the willingness and readiness of those immediately involved to discuss the particular issue before launching into it.

2.   Set the ground rules for carrying on the conversation before starting it.

Elements of a Contract — the Operating Agreement	
Issue	What and Whose? (Step 1)
	Interest/Commitment?
Ground Rules	
Procedures	Who to Include?
	Where to Meet?
	When and for How Long?
How	Talk Openly
	Be Respectful
	Use Tools?
At Any Point	Call Time Out
	Check Process

In Step 2, Specifically Consider:

Procedures:

- *Who* should be, and should not be, included?

  Consider all SOS people. Include key people.

- *Where* will you talk?

  Choose a private place.

  Find a location that fits for everyone.

  Limit distractions.

- *When* will you talk and for how *long*?

  Consider everyone's preferences. Do not force a discussion at the wrong time or you will generate tension and resistance.

  Realize that conversing too long or running out of time before closure are both frustrating and often counterproductive.

How You Will Work:

This element sets the tone. Before beginning a discussion, establish operational expectations to:

- Talk openly about the issue (Styles III and IV).

- Be respectful of one another (Count SOS).

- Determine aids or tools, For example, decide if it is helpful to have a recorder, post the steps of this model, work at a flip chart, or just sit together. (Keep your pocket cards handy for reference, too.)

At any Point:

- Call Time Out. Agree that anyone can call Time Out, for reasons such as:

  Emotions running too high

  Feeling saturated, fatigued

  Wanting to reschedule, or needing more time

Issues do not always need to be resolved at one sitting. Often, time to digest what has been heard or to cool off brings new perspective and resolution. Time Out functions as a safety valve to prevent overheating or information overload.

If Time Out is called, be sure to recontract to discuss the issue further, when the time is right.

- Check Process. Note that briefly stepping back and checking the participants' satisfaction with the process, its pace, or the productivity of the discussion can be useful at any time. To do this, ask questions such as:

  Are we on or off track?

  Are you being understood?

  Should we move ahead (and suggest the next step)?

  Should we stop for now and reschedule?

Contracting itself is a preliminary Check-Process activity.

> Results (outcomes) rarely exceed the quality of your contract — the operating agreement.

Keep in mind:

- If the parties to an issue are never willing to get together to work out a resolution, the contract itself (and sometimes the future of the relationship) becomes the primary issue.
- It only takes one element of the contract to be out of sync to dampen the process of working through an issue effectively.
- Generally, you will find that establishing ground rules increases each person's involvement.

Suggestions About Ground Rules

- Realize that running down this list each time you want to deal with an issue is not always necessary. Be aware, however, that some form of an underlying operating agreement — ground rules — runs through every discussion.
- Notice that when everyone is ready and willing — the ground rules are set — a surprising amount can be accomplished, even in a limited time frame.
- Attend to participants' nonverbals prior to, as well as during, the discussion for clues about whether or not your contract to work on the issue is in effect. If you are in doubt, check it out.

Sometimes Identifying the Issue and Contracting (Steps 1 and 2) are preliminary and separate from the actual discussion. Other times they immediately precede the discussion.

STEP 3. UNDERSTAND THE ISSUE COMPLETELY

The purpose of this step is to *develop complete understanding of the issue before taking action*. This prevents pre-closure — jumping quickly to solutions that do not fit.

To understand the issue, use Open Questions and the Attentive Listening skills to encourage the other people involved to talk thoroughly about their experience of the issue. And when they have told their story, you use the talking skills to contribute your point of view. In effect, you help everyone focus on the four questions below:

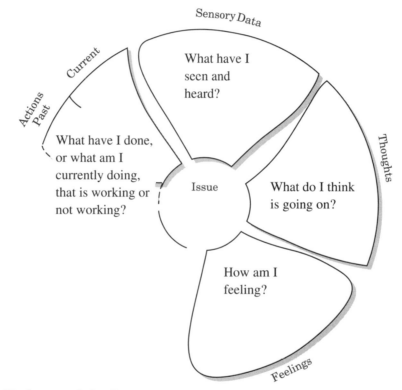

How to Understand the Issue:

■ As each person shares his or her experience with the others, attend to hot and cold responses. Be ready to lead or follow, either as a participant or the facilitator.

■ Keep participants taking turns — focusing on past/current actions, data, thoughts, and feelings — until everyone has had a chance to share all he or she wishes to say.

■ Sometimes this step takes a while. Remember, however, that understanding is the foundation of effective and congruent future action.

Understanding as the Solution

Occasionally you will discover that it is not necessary to go beyond Step 3, because the very process of understanding the issue in itself has become the solution.

STEP 4. IDENTIFY WANTS

This step focuses on the wants of each person, *for* the SOS System, in relation to the issue.

Each needs to determine:

- What do I want *for Self?*
- What do I want *for Other(s)* — the people *centrally* involved?
- What do I want *for* the *Stakeholders* — the people *peripherally* involved yet still affected?

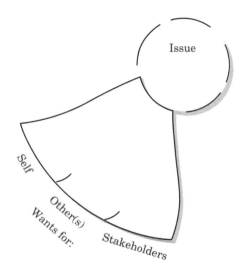

- Be careful that confusion does not exist between what the participants want *for* others, with what they want *from* others. (Note that what they want *from* others goes under wants *for* self.)
- Recycle everyone's wants for other(s) after you have heard everyone's wants for self. (Sometimes you do not know what you want for others until you have heard them say what they want for themselves.)
- Include *don't wants* as well as *wants.*

The Key to Collaboration

In resolving conflicts, this step on wants is absolutely critical. To affirm and to build on the wants of others (as well as on one's own wants) is central to success in collaborating.

STEP 5. GENERATE AND CONSIDER OPTIONS

At this point participants in the conversation *brainstorm what they could actually do to resolve the issue,* or at least move it ahead.

First, Generate Options:

■ Brainstorm a diverse list of small positive actions that anyone involved can actually take as next steps rather than try to come up with one big solution.

■ Remember the 80/20 rule — the answers are primarily inside SOS — the people involved.

■ Keep in view the participants' expanded understanding of the issue (Step 3).

■ Take into account wants *for SOS* (Step 4).

■ Be sure to include both new possibilities that have not been tried and past actions that have been helpful. (Do not repeat what is not working.)

■ Generate possibilities without pausing to critique the options.

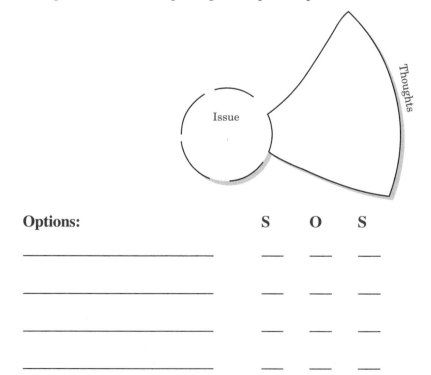

Next, Consider the Impact of Each Potential Action on the SOS System:

■ Consider the worst and best outcome that could happen with each action.

■ Draw an arrow up ↑, down ↓, or up and down — mixed ↑ ↓ to estimate the fit of each option for every SOS person.

STEP 6. CHOOSE ACTIONS

Choose Best-Fit Action(s) to Implement:

- Synthesize and combine actions if you wish (from Step 5).
- Choose options that are the most workable and beneficial for the SOS System.

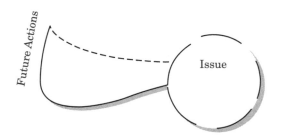

- Confirm who will do what by when.

Future Action Plan

Who Will Do What?	*By When?*
_____	_____
_____	_____
_____	_____
_____	_____

STEP 7. TEST THE ACTION PLAN

After an action plan is chosen, test it by pausing for a moment and having you and any participants imagine yourselves — SOS — actually carrying out the actions.

- If each of you sees, hears, and experiences yourself and others following through with each action effectively, and feels satisfied, great! Your plans fits.

- However, if anyone cannot see himself or herself or others carrying out the action plan, or feels dissatisfied with the outcome, consider where interference occurs. Does *sensory data,* a *thought, feeling, want,* or *action* exist that does not fit congruently and that dampens the plan? If so, talk about it. Revise the action plan, taking the incongruent part into account.

- Perhaps the incongruency or dissatisfaction signals a new issue. The zone of the Awareness Wheel in which you are stuck may be signaling a different or deeper issue that is really blocking resolution of the original issue. If time and energy are not available immediately to map and resolve the new issue, contract to deal with the new issue later.

STEP 8. EVALUATE THE OUTCOME

After you have had a chance to act, evaluate your plan and determine how well it worked. (If this issue was one in which you facilitated others, you will need to check with those people about the outcome.)

If your action has been effective, you will feel pleased. Celebrate!

If your action has not been effective, you may experience a range of negative feelings — disappointment, frustration, even embarrassment.

- Determine what you have learned from the experience, and generate a new action plan. (Re-map the issue.)

- Do not keep repeating actions that do not work.

Considerations:

- If the planned action was never taken, think about if this is part of a *float* pattern?

- Consider how high involvement (raised expectations) with no follow-through is very demoralizing to SOS.

BENEFITS OF MAPPING ISSUES

Mapping an Issue provides a comprehensive structure for making decisions, solving problems, and resolving conflicts. The process helps you to:

- Think systemically by incorporating the diverse interests of all SOS participants.
- Keep focus on the central issue.
- Diagnose where you are in dealing with an issue, and provide direction for making interventions to guide or facilitate the process.
- Include powerful feelings and wants (typically unacknowledged in many situations).
- Prevent the effects of partial information.
- Make the implicit, explicit and more resolvable.
- Generate congruent, effective solutions.
- Feel satisfied with both the process and the outcome.

This process incorporates all 11 core talking and listening skills to help you and others work through an important issue in a collaborative way.

GUIDELINES FOR FACILITATING THE PROCESS WHEN OTHERS DO NOT KNOW THE SKILLS

- Be clear about your role as counselor/facilitator. Clarify and gain participants' approval for your role (participant-facilitator or non-participant counselor-facilitator).
- Do not minimize or underplay the contract. Be sure to establish the details of an informal operating agreement.
- (Optional) Overview what you are going to do — the Mapping process. Consider usefulness of telling participants at the outset (part of contracting step, perhaps) that you are following a specific process. Most often however, if your role is clear and accepted as the counselor/facilitator, you can lead people confidently through the process without outlining the process beforehand. Usually they are not interested in how you proceed as long as the issue is resolved effectively.
- Monitor each participant's involvement (hot and cold) and contribution, as well as the overall progress of the group.
- Watch readiness to move the process along (either forwards, shifting to the next step, or occasionally backwards if an important step or information seems missing).
- Adjust time in each step to be able to complete the entire process in the time allotted. If more time seems to be needed, Check Process, call Time Out, and reschedule a time to complete the process.

EXERCISE: PRACTICE MAPPING AN ISSUE ONE-ON-ONE

To do the process, consider yourself to be a:

- *Participant* with another individual (who does not know the skills), and you use the Mapping-an-Issue process (as a guide) to facilitate the two of you working out an issue or conflict.

- *Facilitator/Counselor/Consultant* to help another individual (who does not know the skills) to find the best way through his or her difficulty.

Usually, in a real situation, you probably will not use the skills mats. However, in this practice exercise, work with others who do know the skills (lab or workshop setting). Use the mats to prompt yourself "nonlinearly" with the core skills as you "linearly" and sequentially work through an issue using the eight steps.

Instructions for Participant:

1.   Position the skill mats for your (self) use with other, as configured below:

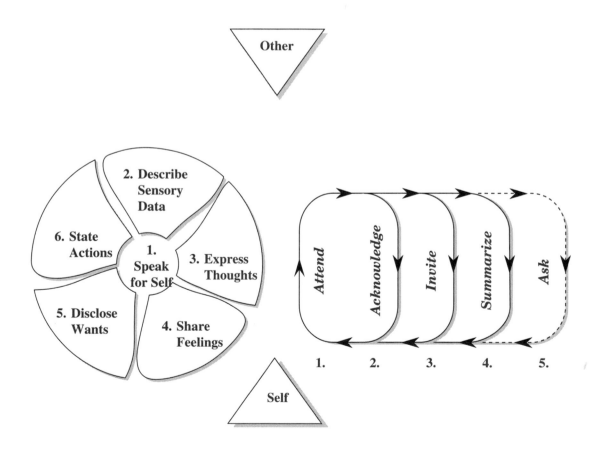

2. Choose a conflict situation that you would have with the other person or for which you could be a counselor.

3. Select someone (in lab or workshop) from a small group to play the role of the surrogate other (to be the person with whom you are having the conflict or the person you are counseling).

4. Briefly give the surrogate enough background information about the real situation so he or she can roleplay the other person relatively accurately.

5. Keep in hand your small Mapping-an-Issue pocket card as a reference to prompt you on the eight steps of the process as you work through the issue. (Also, during the course of the exercise, coach the surrogate on how to play his or her role, if he or she needs help representing the other.)

6. Tell your observer-coaches if you want feedback or not, and advise them on how you would like to be coached.

Instructions for Other (Surrogate)

1. Make sure you have enough information (from the participant) to be able to play the other with relative accuracy and comfort.

2. As you play the role of the surrogate, respond to the participant's behavior as you experience him or her in the interaction. If what he or she is doing is not working, signal cold. On the other hand, if what he or she is doing is working with you, signal warm. (In a simulation like this, it is possible to lock into a role and not respond positively, regardless of how effective the participant's communication is.)

3. Do not hesitate to let yourself be influenced by the participant's actual behavior. He or she is experimenting with new behaviors.

Instructions for Observer Coaches

1. Follow the participant's wishes if you are asked to give feedback and coach. (This is usually most helpful.)

2. Confine your coaching and feedback to *process* — the Core skills, principles, and guides. Do not get sidetracked discussing the *content* or proposing solutions *(outcomes)*.

3. Turn to pages 125-133 in this chapter or use your Mapping-an-Issue pocket card to follow the participant as he or she moves through the eight-steps.

4. Keep this workbook handy to review the points of each step for prompting and feedback.

5. Attend to the Hot and Cold effectiveness of your feedback to the participant you are observing-coaching. Be careful not to over-coach (direct) or flood the participant with too much information. Also be sure to point out things the participant does well.

EXERCISE: PRACTICE MAPPING AN ISSUE WITH OTHERS

To do the process, consider yourself to be a:

- *Facilitator/Mediator* of a group conflict-resolution situation. (Assume they do not know the skills.)

Instructions

A. Contract with the group to serve as their facilitator/mediator. If the group wants you to play this role, continue.

B. As you proceed, use your own full repertoire of core skills as needed to monitor and facilitate the group process.

C. Besides taking the group through the overall structure of the mapping steps, be ready to use the skills to facilitate interactions among members, along the way.

D. Proceed to:

Step 1. Identify and Define the Issue(s)

Step 2. Contract to Work Through the Issue (as a group)

- Consider using a flip chart to structure your facilitation and record the process.

Proceed with the following steps when the group is ready.

Step 3. Understand the Issue Completely

- Attend to hot and cold nonverbals and stop and shift turning points as you watch individual, dyadic, and the group as a whole for your facilitation clues.

- Encourage members to speak for themselves, if you hear them speaking for others.

- If there is considerable misunderstanding, or tension within the group, encourage or direct various group members to summarize each other's statements occasionally, before adding more information.

- Also be aware of members' use of questions. Do not let one group member take over (control) the process with his or her questions.

Step 4. Identify Wants

- Help participants clearly distinguish and cover wants for SOS.

Step 5. Generate and Consider Options

Step 6. Choose Actions

Step 7. Test the Action Plan

Step 8. Evaluate the Outcome

USE OF MAPPING-AN-ISSUE PROCESS

Instructions

Rate your facility with the Mapping-Issues steps below:

	Special Strength	Okay As Is	Work Area
Step 1. Identify and Define the Issue	_____	_____	_____
Step 2. Contract to Work Through the Issue	_____	_____	_____
Step 3. Understand the Issue Completely	_____	_____	_____
Step 4. Identify Wants	_____	_____	_____
Step 5. Generate and Consider Options	_____	_____	_____
Step 6. Choose Action(s)	_____	_____	_____
Step 7. Test the Action Plan	_____	_____	_____
Step 8. Evaluate the Outcome	_____	_____	_____

Action Plan

- Circle two steps to improve.

11

SPECIAL PROCESSES

Responding to:
Fight Talk
Spite Talk
Mixed Messages

NEGATIVE STYLE II COMMUNICATION

Style II communication has tremendous pulling power. This means any hint from one person of a negative Style II message — Fight Talk, Spite Talk or a Mixed Message — usually pulls the other person into Style II, as well. The other person goes into Style II to protect himself or herself by defending or counter-attacking. Style II is very strong.

This section offers processes — built on *Core Communication* skills, principles, and guides — for you to employ to respond more effectively to negative Style II messages. These processes are useful only if your intent is to value and count the SOS system involved.

Each process presented here includes a sequence of steps. Consider them as sub-routines in a larger interaction, the purpose of which is to resolve an issue.

> When you encounter negative Style II, reach for the skills.

RESPONDING TO FIGHT TALK

When someone is using Fight Talk, the person is negatively charged, directly and actively challenging or attacking, you. (See Chapter 1 for a complete description.) Your job is to engage the person (if possible) and rechannel the negative emotion into a productive outcome.

Note: First of all, if you think you are in any physical danger, leave the situation. Get out of harm's way. Protect yourself! In any exchange with an angry person, keep a safe physical distance.

If you choose to engage the person, these are the steps to do so:

1. **Recognize the other person's nonverbal pressure cues.** These include upper body and facial tension, forceful gestures, and strident tone of voice. Also notice the angry words.

2. **Breathe and center.** This lets go of your own negative energy (your tension or muscle strain) and positions you for more centered, flexible responses. Let yourself assume an open, alert, non-defensive posture.

3. **Attend** (Look, Listen, and Track, but do not Mirror, the negative behavior).

4. **Relate first to the person's emotion** as you listen to the other's beliefs, feelings, wants, and actions.

    Acknowledge the other person's emotion (often unstated feeling of anger, fear, or frustration). Then:

    Invite, encourage the person to continue telling his or her full story.

    Summarize the concerns to demonstrate to the person that he or she has been heard accurately (even if you do not agree with what he or she has said).

    This process neutralizes the attacker by going with his or her energy and offering nothing for this challenger to resist.

5. **Watch for warming nonverbals** before you attempt to lead in any way.

6. **Look and Listen for real signs of relieved pressure — no Fight Talk.** Pick up on and complete any unfinished concerns. Continue to deal with the issue in a calm way. Use Straight Talk and Attentive Listening.

Other Potentially Connecting Responses Include:

- Agreeing with what is being said if you honestly can.

- Extending what the person is saying. (For example, "It's worse than what you are saying.")

- Admitting what you have done or what has happened if the person is accurate. (Be accountable.)

- Give genuine credit. (For example, "You're doing me a favor by pointing this out.")

- Joining by sharing (in Straight Talk) your own frustration (not directed at the other) with the situation.

Suggestions

- Do the unexpected — help rather than resist.

- Do not meet a challenger with rational reasons, or tell the person why he or she should not feel that way. You will receive a cold response and escalate the tension.

- Do not move too quickly to leading. Demonstrate understanding and caring before attempting to lead. Do not just say insincerely, "I understand," as a transition to direct the exchange.

- Keep centered. Your relaxed flexible responses will have a calming effect on the other person.

EXERCISE: RESPOND TO FIGHT TALK

1. Recall a situation in which someone used Fight Talk with you. If you could re-do the situation, what would you do, using the process above?

2. Think of a time or a place in which you can apply this process with someone you know who uses Fight Talk with you.

RESPONDING TO SPITE TALK

When someone is using Spite Talk, the person signals a negative, unhappy undercurrent by withholding, resisting, or challenging you passively and indirectly. The Style reflects someone who is lethargic, disengaged, hurt, or angry. (See Chapter 1 for a complete description.) Your job is to connect with the other person in a way that helps energize and focus his or her discontent toward a more congruent and constructive resolution.

A. Recognize the nonverbals (the other person's pressure cues). For example, notice disengaged posture, flat facial expression, lack of eye contact, sighs, and flat or whiny tone of voice. Also notice the cynical words.

B. Breathe and center. Do not be intimidated by the other person's tense silence and anger. Work from your center.

C. Describe what you see and hear, and ask what is wrong. Do not let Spite Talk go unacknowledged. Your description may result in:

- A continued negative response by the person (The more passive and powerless the person is, when angry, the more frequently he or she will deny that anything is wrong.).

- A positive response by the person. (Go directly to Steps 5 and 6 below.)

If you receive a negative response; for instance, you do not get a straight response:

- Choose whether or not to pursue the negativity.

- If not, let it go.

- If so, deal with it using the following steps:

   1. **Do not keep asking what is wrong. Break state.** Do something to get the other to change posture and context, and to breathe. This will physically put him or her in a position to be more responsive. For example, think of an excuse to take a walk together, or get some coffee. Walking or sitting side-by-side also relieves some of the typical face-to-face pressure

   2. **Speak for Self, about the other, demonstrating empathy, if he or she remains silent.** Start by saying that you have been thinking about the other person and describe what you think is going on inside the other person's Wheel. Try to be as accurate about all parts of his or her Wheel as you can.

      Be willing to own in Straight Talk (without being manipulated) anything you have done to contribute to the other person's getting upset.

3. **Watch for small warming nonverbals** that confirm your accuracy as you speak. (Often the person will respond either positively to your empathy or correct your inaccuracy, if you are inaccurate.) Whatever the response, you have helped energize the person to talk about his or her having been wounded. Build on any positive responses.

4. **If you receive no response, do not lapse back into trying to get the other person to talk to you by asking questions.** Rather, end the conversation by saying, "Take your time to think things over and get back to me when you are ready. In the meantime, I'll assume what I have just said (see Step 2) is true for you."

If you receive a positive response, for instance, the person says that something is wrong:

5. **Map the issue together.** (Follow the process model of mapping from Chapter 10 of this workbook.)

6. **Offer choices** and act on his or her wants, if possible.

Considerations:

- Keep in mind that people act with spite when they feel hurt and angry and believe that resentful resistance is the only power they possess.

- Consider having a Straight Talk conversation about the other person's pattern of Spite Talk, asking for change in the behavior.

- Make a decision. When a person continues spiteful behavior after some effort to deal with it on your part, decide to what extent you will continue the relationship and draw boundaries for yourself.

- Set limits and define consequences, if you are in any position of authority over the person, after you have applied the process given above several times. Tell the person that such behavior (be specific and concrete) is unacceptable and must stop or particular consequences will follow.

EXERCISE: RESPOND TO SPITE TALK

1. Recall a situation in which someone used Spite Talk with you. If you could re-do the situation, what would you do, using the process above?

2. Anticipate an occasion for responding to Spite Talk with someone who uses this style with you.

MIXED MESSAGES

Mixed messages include an undercurrent of Style II with any other style.

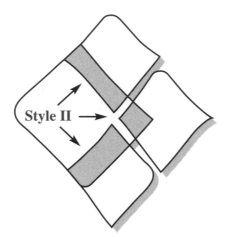

Mixed Messages Come in Three Forms:

- Any style (Small, Shop, Search, or Straight Talk) mixed with *Style II words* (Control, Fight, or Spite Talk). The overall message is contradictory or unclear.

    "I appreciate your thorough job (Straight Talk), but it sure took you forever" (Control or Fight Talk, depending on tone).

- Any style mixed with *Style II nonverbals* (gestures or tone in Fight or Spite Talk). The meaning is contradictory or confusing.

    "I wonder if others on the committee enjoy the benefit of your wisdom." (Words are in Search Talk, but spoken in a cynical-sounding tone, with a slight smile towards someone else.)

- Two contradictory *Style II messages* — one part positive, the other part negative. The meaning is unclear.

    "You're pretty smart for such a dumb guy." (The words are Style II, while the tone is Small-Talk joking. What part is really meant?)

Generally the purer the style is, the clearer the message. Mixed messages send unclear messages.

Typical Impacts of Mixed Messages on the Recipient (and Bystanders, too)

Caution	Distrust	Hurt
Confusion	Embarrassment	Resistance

The negative aspect of the message registers the strongest impact.

Usual Reasons for Mixed Messages:

The talker:

- Is afraid or embarrassed to bring up an issue directly.
- Has mixed feelings in relation to the recipient.
- Is not in touch with or unclear about his or her self-awareness (Wheel).
- Does not know how to give clear messages.
- Does not know or care about the impact of the message on the recipient.
- Has an issue with the recipient.

Responding to Mixed Messages

Comment on both parts of the contradictory message, or at least acknowledge the negative part. Consider asking which part the talker really means. For example:

> Mixed Message: "I think your talk can go well (Small Talk context), but knowing you, it won't" (Spite Talk).

> Response: "I'm hearing conflicting messages. Which do you mean, that I'll do a good job or that I'll mess up?"

EXERCISE: CLEARING THE MIXED MESSAGE

Think of some mixed messages you have heard. Then write your response, including a question about which part the talker means.

Mixed Message:

Response:

Mixed Message:

Response:

Mixed Message:

Response:

Generalizations About Styles

- People resort to Fight and Spite Talk when they think they are being discounted.

- Style II is a powerful style. It can overpower Style I, Style III, and even other Style II talking or listening behaviors.

- Only Style IV is paradoxically more powerful than Style II. This is the paradox: When a person is trying to be powerful in Style II, he or she is not. When a person is not trying to be powerful in Style IV, he or she is powerful. As soon as someone tries to use Style IV to be powerful, he or she slips into Style II communication — verbally or nonverbally — and gives up his or her real power.

- The power in Style IV comes from managing self and not trying to control other(s).

- It does not work to use Straight Talk or Attentive Listening to fake a caring attitude or a desire to be collaborative, if neither is true. Others see and hear the incongruent nonverbals, signaling a desire to control (Style II), and begin to distrust the person.

- Style IV is influential. Disclosure (in Style IV) attracts disclosure.

- In Style IV, you can try directly to influence the other, saying your intentions. Yet you leave the choice with the other. When you slip into coercing, you are in Style II. (If your intention is to be in control, say so. Your disclosure of that intention is using Straight Talk, Style IV, which gives the other the choice to go along with you or not.)

- Knowing the communication styles increases your choices in how to deal with issues, which is particularly important when you are under stress or when a conflict arises.

12

PLANNING A PROCESS

**Analyze Situation
Plan Your Process
Figure Contingencies
Take Action**

ANTICIPATING A CONVERSATION

When you know that you have an issue to resolve with someone and want a conversation about it to go well, you can plan ahead of time for the interaction. This section will help you develop a process for such a situation. As you do so, you can draw upon any of the following:

- Four Maps
- Six Talking and Five Listening Skills
- Six Interactive Principles
- Five Interactive Guides
- General, Collaborative, and Special Processes

(A more detailed review is listed on the next page.)

The purpose of making and carrying out this plan is to help you (and whoever else is involved) feel satisfied with both the process of dealing with the issue and the outcome of it, whatever its content. Also, as you anticipate and then actually put your plan into effect, it is likely that you will gain more confidence in your use of these various aspects of communication.

CORE COMMUNICATION MENU

Four Maps

The Communication Styles The Listening Cycle
The Awareness Wheel   Conflict Patterns

Six Talking and Five Listening Skills

Speak for Self   Attend: Look, Listen, Track
Describe Sensory Data   Acknowledge Other's Experience
Express Thoughts   Invite More Information
Share Feelings   Summarize to Ensure Accuracy
Disclose Wants   Ask Open Questions
State Actions

Six Interactive Principles

Issues affect parts and whole (SOS).
Your behavior and attitude reflect one another.
Issues indicate something is changing or must change.
When demands appear to exceed available resources to cope, stress
 increases.
Every body speaks its mind — nonverbally.
Resistance is your guide.

Five Interactive Guides

Use your awareness.
Breathe and center.
Establish and maintain rapport.
Play Hot or Cold — Ask yourself, "Is what I am doing working or not
 working?"
Recognize, stop and shift.

Three Major Processes

General — Lead and Follow
Collaborative — Map an Issue
Special — Respond to Negative Style II

PLAN A PROCESS

For this plan, choose an important, complicated, or stressful issue that you want to work out with one other person. (The general planning can also fit times for involving several people, but to make it manageable at this point, figure for just the two of you in the conversation.) Your task is to anticipate and prepare for a skilled conversation (with a caring attitude) with the person about the issue.

Four basic steps make up your plan. This is the overview.

Step 1. Do An Analysis. In this analysis, figure out:

What the issue is and with whom; who else in the SOS system is involved.

Awareness about the issue for yourself, and the other person.

What you consider a satisfactory outcome to be.

Step 2. Develop Your Interaction Plan. Determine:

Whether you will establish a contract for the conversation.

A brief preamble to set the tone for the conversation.

What you intend to do in sequence (generally) and the skills and processes you will use.

Any prompts to use (such as notes or pocket cards).

Step 3. Anticipate Process Contingencies — How to respond to the Unexpected. Decide:

What could go wrong in the interaction; what to keep in mind for yourself that would help you (such as principles or guides that you could let slip).

What would be the cues that things are not going right.

What the person might do to throw you off track.

What guides, skills, or processes you will use to recover.

Step 4. Rehearse Your Process.

If you do so in front of others who know the skills and processes, decide if you want coaching and feedback on your rehearsal.

If you are alone, actually use the floor skills mats to walk through the sequence, or close your eyes and imagine yourself carrying out the process. Go through the whole process, part by part.

Directions: Use the worksheets below to analyze and plan your conversation.

Step 1. Do An Analysis.

- What is the issue?

- Who is the Other person?

- Besides you (Self) and the Other person, who are the Stakeholders?

- Fill out the Awareness Wheel below for yourself in relation to the issue.

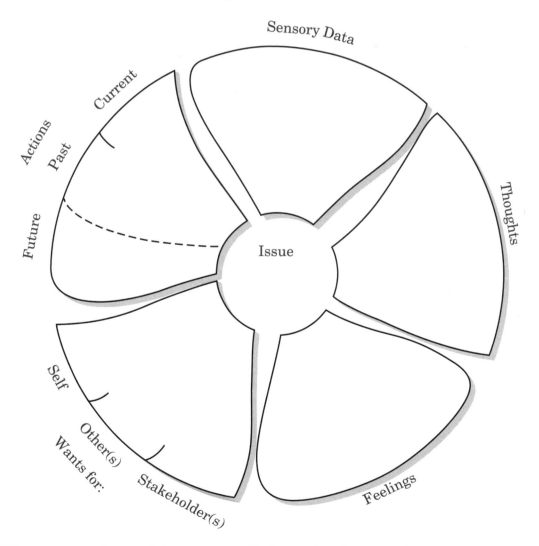

- What awareness of yourself do you want to disclose to the other person?

EXERCISE

- Stand in the Other person's shoes. Fill out the Awareness Wheel as you think it is, from that person's perspective about the issue. To do this, recall what you have seen the other person do and heard him or her say. Add anything else that fits from other sensory data you have about the person.

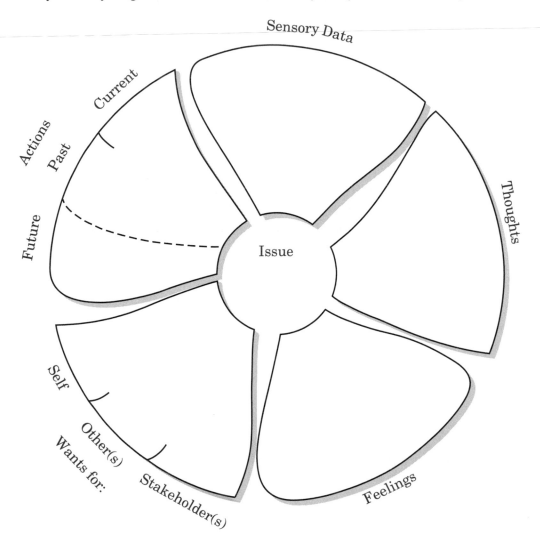

- Look at both Wheels. What information seems particularly significant?

- What wants do you have in common that you are aware of now?

- What information is missing from the other person's Wheel (because you just do not know what it is)? Is this something to discover when you meet?

- From what you are aware of at this point, what would be a satisfactory outcome for everyone in the SOS System?

Step 2. Develop Your Interaction Plan.

■ Consider whether you will you establish a contract for the conversation (develop an operating agreement)? What ground rules would you include? (See pages 126-128 for contracting.)

■ When your conversation actually begins, what brief preamble will you use to set the tone for the conversation?

■ Based on the Self and Other Awareness Wheels you have completed, how will you proceed with the discussion? (For example, proceed by leading — sharing the zones of your Wheel in some particular order or by asking an open question? Or, proceed by following — inviting the other to talk?) List your anticipated sequence of processes and skills below: (Look on page 148 for possibilities.)

1. _____

2. _____

3. _____

4. _____

5. _____

■ List anything particularly important to keep in mind for yourself in the situation that would help you (such as principles or guides).

■ Write any prompts to use (such as notes, pocket cards).

Step 3. Anticipate Process Contingencies — How to respond to the Unexpected.

■ What could go wrong in the interaction or get things off track?

■ List your process contingencies (for example, stop/shift, follow resistance, breathe/center):

_____

_____

_____

_____

Step 4. Rehearse Your Process.

■ If you are with others who have learned the *Core Communication Skills and Processes*, who can also serve as observer-coaches, share your plan with them. Let them know the issue, the intended sequence and your set of contingencies. Ask one of them to be a surrogate of the person you have the issue with, as you rehearse your process. The others in the group can be observers. Let them know if you want any coaching or, when you complete the rehearsal, any feedback.

■ If you are alone, actually use the floor skills mats to walk through the sequence, or close your eyes and imagine yourself carrying out all parts of the process. When you run into difficulties as you imagine, then recall the contingencies.

In either case:

■ Imagine yourself, managing yourself — staying in the zone of being: **centered and aware, present and engaging** as you resolve the issue with the other person.

TAKE ACTION — CARRY OUT THE PROCESS.

Afterwards: Reflect on How it Went

- What was the process like for you and for the other?

- What do you think you did well?

- What could you improve?

- What is your level of satisfaction (with the process, with the outcome)?

- What do you think the satisfaction level is for the other person and for any stakeholders?

POST-QUESTIONNAIRE: SKILLS AND PROCESSES

Date_____

Instructions

Without reviewing how you marked your pre-questionnaire, follow the three steps below to assess how you are currently communicating, and to determine how well you have achieved your learning goals.

Step 1. Mark each item twice: first with an "X" to represent your typical behavior and again with an "O" to represent your more-so- or less-so desired behavior. If your typical and desired behaviors are the same, the "X" and "O" marks will be on the same number. If they are not the same, the marks will fall on different numbers.

In general, when you are discussing an issue with someone, how often do you:

	Seldom Often	Difference
1. Direct or instruct the other in what to do about it?	1 2 3 4 5 6	___
2. Blame or attack the other directly?	1 2 3 4 5 6	___
3. Send clear, complete, and straightforward messages?	1 2 3 4 5 6	___
4. Make spiteful, undercutting remarks indirectly?	1 2 3 4 5 6	___
5. Explore possible causes of the issue?	1 2 3 4 5 6	___
6. Speak for other — put words into the other's mouth?	1 2 3 4 5 6	___
7. Use your full awareness to reflect on the issue?	1 2 3 4 5 6	___
8. Share your feelings?	1 2 3 4 5 6	___
9. Disclose your wants and desires?	1 2 3 4 5 6	___
10. Calm yourself consciously when you feel tense or encounter tension in the other	1 2 3 4 5 6	___
11. Establish and maintain rapport?	1 2 3 4 5 6	___
12. Listen briefly, then begin talking?	1 2 3 4 5 6	___
13. Attend to the other's nonverbal responses?	1 2 3 4 5 6	___
14. Acknowledge the other's feelings?	1 2 3 4 5 6	___
15. Acknowledge the wants and desires of the other?	1 2 3 4 5 6	___
16. Invite/encourage the other to expand on a point of view?	1 2 3 4 5 6	___
17. Ask what the other is thinking, feeling, and wanting?	1 2 3 4 5 6	___

	Seldom	Often	Difference
18. Summarize messages of the other to ensure accuracy?	1 2 3 4 5 6		___
19. Avoid the issue by joking or changing the subject?	1 2 3 4 5 6		___
20. Force decisions on the other?	1 2 3 4 5 6		___
21. Give in to the other's decision?	1 2 3 4 5 6		___
22. Talk about the issue but leave it unresolved?	1 2 3 4 5 6		___
23. Settle the issue by compromising — trading for something?	1 2 3 4 5 6		___
24. Resolve the issue by building agreements collaboratively?	1 2 3 4 5 6		___
25. Identify clearly what the issue is before discussing it?	1 2 3 4 5 6		___
26. Begin a discussion without considering the other's readiness?	1 2 3 4 5 6		___
27. Propose a good time and place to discuss the issue?	1 2 3 4 5 6		___
28. Decide upon a solution before fully hearing the concern?	1 2 3 4 5 6		___
29. Brainstorm solutions to the issue?	1 2 3 4 5 6		___
30. Make sure a solution to the issue fits well for everyone involved?	1 2 3 4 5 6		___

Total Difference Score ___

Step 2. When you have completed marking all the items, calculate the numerical difference between typical and desired scores for each item and record the results in the "difference" column. If the "X" and "O" are on the same number, the difference = 0. If the "X" is on 5 and the "O" is on 2, the difference = 3. Note the the "O" can be located on a higher or lower number than the "X." Do not be concerned about the higher or lower direction of the scores, just calculate the numerical difference between the marks.

Step 3. Sum the difference scores. (See the next page to review your skill learning.)

REVIEW YOUR SKILL LEARNING

When you have completed scoring your Post-Questionnaire, turn to your Pre-Questionnaire located in the Preface to *Core Communication*. Consider the following:

1. Determine how well you have achieved the learning goals you set for yourself on the Pre-Questionnaire.

2. Compare any changes in the "Total Difference Scores" from pre- to Post-Questionnaires.

   A lower score (from pre- to post- questionnaire) indicates that you have progressed closer to your desired skill use.

   A higher score (from pre- to post- questionnaire) indicates that you have moved further away from your desired skill use.*

For Your Information

In the Pre- and Post-Questionnaires, items 1 - 5 relate to Chapter 1, Communication Styles Map; items 6 - 9 relate to Chapter 3, The Awareness Wheel Map and Talking Skills; item 10 relates to Chapter 4, Interactive Principles and Guides; item 11 relates to Chapter 5, Interactive Principles and Guides; items 12 - 18 relate to Chapter 6, The Listening Map and Skills; items 19 - 24 relate to Chapter 9, Conflict Patterns Map; items 25 - 30 relate to Chapter 10, Collaborative Process: Mapping an Issue.

* If you have an increase in your Post-Questionnaire Difference Score, here are two reasons this can happen. (1) You may be using more skills now, yet you also realize how much more effectively you could use the skills. In other words, your awareness has changed, and you have higher expectations of what skill use involves. (2) You may not have achieved the skill-learning progress you desired. If this is true, you may wish to consult with your *Core Communication* instructor about your results.

ABOUT THE AUTHORS

Sherod Miller, Ph.D. is Chairman of Interpersonal Communication Programs, Inc. He is co-author of the best sellers: *Alive and Aware* and *Straight Talk*, and well known for his work in interpersonal communication and team development. He is a seasoned clinician, teacher, and organizational effectiveness trainer-consultant to a number of major corporations. He is a former Research Associate at the Family Study Center and faculty member in the Department of Medicine at the University of Minnesota. He has received two national awards for his research and teaching.

Phyllis A. Miller, Ph. D. is President of Interpersonal Communication Programs, Inc. She is co-author of *Talking and Listening Together, Collaborative Team Skills,* and *Connecting With Self and Others.* In addition to the books on interpersonal communication, she has authored *Managing Your Reading* and materials for *Flexible Reading,* a video series she taught, appearing for a number of years on public television. She has been on the staff at the University of Minnesota and at Augsburg College in Minneapolis. She is a consultant-facilitator in communication-related areas to business and non-profit organizations.

OTHER RESOURCES

If you have found the *Core Communication* program useful, consider these other related programs and materials from Interpersonal Communication Programs, Inc. (ICP)

Collaborative Team Skills

This program teaches groups who work together the same maps, skills, and processes that *Core Communication* offers to individuals. Participants use their own and their group's real issues as they learn how to communicate about situations and resolve conflicts more effectively. *Collaborative Team Skills* is useful in the following contexts:

■ Team Building

■ Staff Development

■ Implementation of Self-Directed Work Teams

Couple Communication

This program teaches couples the same maps, skills, and processes as in this workbook for individuals. The purpose is to help partners communicate better about day-to-day issues and resolve their conflicts, so that they can build a more satisfying relationship. *Couple Communication* is offered in two ways:

■ As an individual couple

■ In a group with up to 12 couples

Names of certified instructors are available by state from ICP, or see www.couplecommunication.com

If you want to read more:

The book *Connecting With Self and Others* offers a comprehensive yet practical look at communication and relationships. It provides in-depth discussions of the maps, skills, and processes of this workbook and adds others, for example, on phases of relationship, individual similarities and differences, and the interpersonal dance.

A separate *Connecting Skills Workbook* is a companion to the book. It contains exercises for practice and application of the concepts and skills presented in the book.

For a catalog about these programs and other materials, contact:

Interpersonal Communication Programs, Inc.
Suite 200
30772 Southview Drive
Evergreen, CO 80439
Phone: 1-800-328-5099
303-674-2051   FAX: 303-674-4283